Rinus Michels

Team Building
the road to success

Reedswain Publishing

originally published by Uitgeverij Eisma bv, Leeuwarden, The Netherlands
© Copyright 2001

Editing support: TS Tekst, Tjeu Seeverens, Gulpen NL
Tekst Top, Henny Kormelink, Nieuwstadt NL
Translation: Jerome and Miriam Hickey, Almere, The Netherlands
Photography: Bob Friedlander, Jan de Koning, Paul Röling, Tekst Top,
Voetbal International, Leo Vogelzang et al.

**Library of Congress
Cataloging - in - Publication Data**

by Rinus Michels
Team Building - the road to success

ISBN No. 1-890946-73-7
Lib. of Congress Catalog No. 2001119628
© 2001

Editing
Bryan R. Beaver

Reedswain Publishing
88 Wells Road
Spring City, PA 19475
800.331.5191
www.reedswain.com
info@reedswain.com

Contents

*It is my privilege to dedicate this book
to Vera Pauw and Bert van Lingen.
They were invaluable in the development
of this book.*

FOREWORD

In this book, I have made an effort to describe my experiences as a trainer-coach of youth teams, amateur teams and professional teams in a structural manner. At all these levels, however different in environment, intensity and the way the game is experienced by the players, one central theme can be recognized: the influencing of the performance level in a positive way.

To achieve this, the trainer has three different elements at his disposal: the quality of the player pool, the match mentality, and the team building mechanism. The starting point is of course the group of players you work with. Every player has his own personality and living environment. Every one of them desires preferential treatment within the team. Intuitively every player is a proponent of certain team tactics that lets him shine. They all love to play the game, but all players differ in how far they will, and can go to try to win.

These many little "kingdoms" have to be melted in to one team, with the willingness to bundle all the available resources to battle the common "enemy". Only one person can achieve this: the trainer! He has a complicated dual role. At one side he has to respect each little "kingdom" and on the other side he has to win over all the players, so they will sacrifice themselves for the common goal: the result of the match. This dual role controls his daily life.

This phenomenon is called Team Building. It is the most important tool in improving and guarding the achievement level of the team. One coach uses this tool in an intuitive manner as a result of his practical experience. Another coach makes an effort to work as structurally as possible. Personally, I have learned to look at team building as a step by step process.

Especially over the past ten years, the top level of professional football has been characterized by a development in collectively defending, which places high demands on individual and team qualities during build-up and attack. In light of my many experiences, I have made an effort with this book to put forward tools to make the complex team building process come to life, in the pursuit of raising the performance level.

CHAPTER 1

General Introduction

In between my videotape collection of match analyses and successful games of Ajax, FC Barcelona and the Dutch national team stands a tape in which the approach of world famous conductor Bernstein is described. It shows how Bernstein starts a rehearsal with a philharmonic orchestra from America. The one musician is even better than the other is. The absolute best in the world. The conductor asks all members of the orchestra to play a piece from their musical arrangement. He listens with concentration, and only nods every now and then. After a few minutes Bernstein analyzes, using carefully chosen words, what he has heard. "Individually you are all very accomplished, but as an orchestra you will have to travel a long and difficult road. You think you have achieved the ultimate level, but perfection in an orchestra can be taken from ninety-five to one hundred percent."

Football coaches have often been compared to conductors. Every musician plays his own role and instrument in an orchestra. It is not only the task of the conductor to ensure that every one of the individual musicians is able to contribute, he must also ensure that the result is harmonic. It is the most important prerequisite to achieve a unique performance, which is greater than the sum of the individual achievements of all musicians together. The audience has the sense that the music flows effortlessly. Only then has the highest level of performance been reached! This is true as much for a local philharmonic orchestra as for a world famous philharmonic orchestra under the direction of a top-notch conductor.

You can probably make the comparison with the tasks of a football coach yourself. A coach must also create a team out of eleven individual players, who together are making an effort to reach the highest possible level. But you can only take the comparison so far. I dare to say that the job of a conductor is easier than the job of a top-notch football coach. During a match a team is under constant pressure by the opponent, who are doing everything within their power to disrupt the play of the other team. There is a continuous change in the possession of the ball between the teams. In contrast with the musicians who can remain seated and concentrate on their musical contribution and the conductor, football players are constantly confronted with movements all around them. A book in which every play is described, as on sheet music, does not exist for football.

During a ninety-minute match every player constantly has to anticipate the ever-changing situations and make split second decisions about which option to take. They are created by the actions of team-mates and opponents. The true top-notch players all possess the quality to continuously and quickly oversee all the possible options. They also have the technical abilities and swift movement patterns to come up with the correct solution in most situations. The coach prefers team efficient solutions. These solutions will express directly or indirectly the aim of the match: to win or at least not to lose. The complexity and unpredictability of the ever-changing situations prevent the perfect match from ever being played. This is a positive fact, it is this unpredictability factor of the game, that is the reason why football is worldwide the most popular sport. It is a given of course, that every coach, especially those at the highest level, strive for perfection to get the most out of their team. The qualities of his players decide what the limits are of the achievement of his team.

The strive for perfection is getting tougher all the time. During the past fifteen years many changes have occurred. The pressures of the commercial interest and the constant media attention have become greater and greater. You are not allowed to lose a match, because of the enormous interests. At the least, you have to conform to the success expectations of the club you are employed by. A top-notch European club will have to qualify for the Champions League, whereas a top amateur club can not afford to be relegated.

The commercial interests are proportionately greater at the professional level. However, the pressure to succeed has become greater at both top level amateur and professional football clubs. Athletic success is not an isolated fact anymore. Success is essential, for example, for participating in international competitions, or for a club at the regional or national level being able to attract sponsors. The support of sponsors after all guarantees a bigger budget and better facilities. Because of that, in every match both teams are under more pressure than ever before.

A higher budget increases after all the possibility to buy better players, hire better qualified staff, and optimize the youth development program. A chain reaction occurs!

This is why, over the past years, on all fronts, clubs have striven to raise the grade of perfection concerning the performance level of the team. More than anything, in this demanding athletic climate, team defensive performance has greatly improved. As a result, higher demands are put forward on build-up and attacking qualities, in individual as well as in team tactics. The individual top-notch players can not be improved much. However, much can be gained from improving their functioning within the team. A structural learning process for players between the ages of 6 -18 and 18-21 is needed now more than ever, to fully ensure the complete development of both the individual abilities and team tactical awareness of the players.

At the top level, the cohesiveness of the team as a whole has become more and more decisive. There is especially room for improving teamwork to raise the performance level. It is then understandable that coaches wish to study all factors that influence the results of the team. The world of football needs a set of rules that form a framework for the process of team building. Through analyzing many matches one learns to understand how the team building mechanism works, and how it can be positively and negatively influenced. Over the past years, I have been intensively studying this phenomenon. It was of great value to have the experiences as a coach of top teams for 27 years. This book is a medium through which I am trying to share my knowledge and experiences with my fellow coaches.

TYPES OF TEAM BUILDING

Teamwork is as old as the game of football itself. The coaches at the present time are not inventing anything new. But, because of the rapid development of the game, and the increased interests which put more pressure on players and coaches, it is a logical step that at the top level structural means are being sought out which will help each player to perform at a higher level, individually and within the team. The high difficulty level of football at the professional level demands this. Video recordings of for example, the Brazilian team during the 1970 World Cup and of the great Dutch team during the 1974 championship, show that the pace, speed of action, and the defensive pressure cannot be compared to the present day game. Players had much more space in those days!

THE PSYCHOLOGICAL TEAM BUILDING PROCESS

In the football world, it is apparent that most coaches think of team building in mental or psychological terms. For example, the mentality of the players and team spirit. They are, of course, essential. Only with these as the basis, is it possible to perfect team tactics. The better the mentality of the players, the better the environment is for the coach to work on the tactical team building process. Also essential is the players' willingness or readiness to work on team tactics in training so as to bring them to life as efficiently as possible in a match (in combination with a winners mentality, of course).

This willingness cannot be taken for granted, it is not a constant factor. It is always under pressure by internal as well as external elements. The motivation to collectively optimize the level of performance cannot be separated from the individual mentality to win at all costs. That winner mentality has a positive influence on the willingness to collectively work to achieve a common goal.

With the psychological team building process every coach must realize this statement is true: 'what works today, is not guaranteed to work tomorrow'. In this domain, there are no guarantees. Therefore the coach must continually remain alert. Every day there can be internal or external factors that can influence the team mentality of the players. This causes a constant change of the tension level. Whenever the team has lost a match or won unexpectedly the day before, the coach must be on the lookout today for the influence it will have on the mental attitude of the players. Thus you cannot say: "last week I handled the group in this way, so I should be able to handle them in the same manner again this week".

In another instance, caution is needed to guard against external factors. If a member of the club management or a player has made nonsensical remarks to the press, you must as coach be very alert for the eventual reactions. This is also true, for example, the moment players are confronted with private problems. They can have a tremendous influence over the functioning of the player at the club.

Another important external factor can be the transfer policy of a club. Think about the far-reaching consequences trainer Morten Olsen had to deal with when Frank and Ronald de Boer were forced to remain with Ajax against their wishes in the '98/'99 season, instead of being allowed to be transferred to FC Barcelona.

The tension, or of course the absence of it, in the period before the next match surely has an impact on the psychological team building process.

The same holds true also for positive and negative developments within the game. Each coach must deal with the internal and external factors relating to team spirit. Dealing with these factors adequately sometimes requires tact from the coach, sometimes harshness, and always consistent, clear and honest behavior.

THE TEAM TACTICAL TEAM BUILDING PROCESS

Many coaches believe that working on the mentality of players is synonymous with team building. At least as important is the team building in regards to how football is played, the team tactical aspects. All coaches work on developing team tactics, but many do not identify or acknowledge it as a structural process. It is more often seen as a form of game tactic, which is important, of course, provided that it is based upon an optimally developed playing style. This requires structural training work using clear, team tactical guidelines. I have broken it down into three distinct types:

ORGANIZATIONAL TEAM BUILDING

Organizational team building concerns the guidelines, which play a role in the team organization, the team structure, and the organizational form. These guidelines define the role and function of every player within the team organization. You can compare them with traffic rules, whereby the individual behavior on the road is 'steered' via the guidelines (the traffic rules) in relation to the other road-users, to prevent a traffic chaos. This conduct through experience becomes automatic. You no longer have to think about it.

This is true for many things on the pitch. There is no time to think. Action must be taken fast and in a team efficient manner. Because in and through this combination the players make each other perform better.

STRATEGICAL TEAM BUILDING

Strategical team building concerns a series of guidelines which describe how within a certain team structure, the whole team, a line or a group of players, defend, build-up, and attack. Important therefore is the continuous positioning of the players in relation to each other, taking into account the resistance of the opponent and the developments in the match.

TACTICAL TEAM BUILDING

Tactical team building concerns such questions as: how do I prepare my team tactically for the up coming match? Should I adjust to the opponent? What kind of influence do the league standings have on the importance of the match?

Which variations do I use, taking the developments in the match into account? They are variations of familiar team strategies. They are based upon specific resistances from a match.

The splitting up of the team building process in three distinct types is of course a schematic approach. In practice, the three distinct types overlap and are intertwined with each other. They are components of each other. This classification must be seen as a frame of reference, as a better foothold for coaches. Depending on the performance level of a team, one coach will use it very much and the next coach will use it less often. Hopefully this book can contribute to the realization by coaches that such a frame of reference is necessary.

In the following chapters I will use practical examples to address with greater depth the team building process inside and outside the pitch. In addition, Chapter 3 will give an in-depth application of the guidelines for the tactical team building process.

COMPLEXITY

The team building process within a football team is particularly comprehensive because of the complexity of the world's most popular sport! There is a clear relationship between the complexity (call it the degree of difficulty), and the high quality demand placed on players within a perfectly cohesive team. Through a number of examples, I shall try to make the degree of complexity more clear. I will discuss sport in general and the game of football specifically.

Naturally, team building also plays an essential role in the business world, but in that setting, time and space factors are harder to define. In sport, matches are always characterized by set time and space factors. The effect of the team building mechanism is therefore more easily measured in sport than in the business world. There is a good reason that business management is very interested in the methods and ideas of team building experts out of the sports world. At the end of chapter of 4 this will be looked at more closely.

FACTORS

The complexity of the team building process within a sport discipline depends for example, amongst other factors, also on the size of the teams. A coach from a rowing team will have to agree that the teamwork for the eight is more complex than for the coxless two. A game of 4v4 is less complicated than 11v11.

Another important factor is the role of every individual within the team. Within top teams in the sport of football it is more widely expected of each player that he is more versatile. Beyond his basic tasks in the position where he plays: defender, midfielder or attacker, he has to posses a surplus value in the other facets of the game. Other sports do not demand such a high level of versatility. During an American football match a total separate team will step on the field when in possession of the ball and when defending. Most sports have the luxury of one or more time-outs, and in ice hockey and basketball, players can be substituted in and out at will. On the other hand, the game of football is based on continuous action! There were times in England when there were no substitutions allowed at all.

There is no other team sport in which the demands placed on individual qualities of players can be as decisive as in the game of football. The high level of complexity, the continuing action, and the continuous change in attacking and defending, guarantee a high level of unpredictability in the ever-changing situations. That alone demands a lot of insight in the game and football intelligence of each player. In American football, but also in other sports, tactical situations for the team can be rehearsed over and over again. Coaches indoctrinate these patterns. Not the unpredictability, but the predictability dominates these sports. In football this is true when a corner kick has to be taken, that is the reason these situations are called set-plays. These situations can be rehearsed under supervision of a coach. This is done constantly in American football. To realize this, each team has several coaches, each with their own specialty. They decide which play to run. In sport tactical terms, we call American football a coaching sport discipline.

In football matches this cannot be realized because of the unpredictability of the situations. The players themselves are the directors. Only they can solve the situations while improvising. We call football a players' sport discipline.

It is essential for each player to develop the extra quality to come up with the most team efficient solution. Each player has to learn to see the tactical connection. The tactical framework put forward by the coach facilitates this learning process.

In the game of American football there is only one player, the quarterback, who must, just like a football player, decide which option is the most team efficient one. The better the protection by his lineman, the longer the time for him to make the correct decision. The quarterback is the team's tactical leader on the pitch. The actions of most other players on the field are orchestrated by set patterns.

This can absolutely not be said about football! The unpredictability of the situations and the constant change of possession and possession by the opponent, demand quarterback qualities from all players. The more options and solutions the player observes in the ever changing situation, the bigger the chance that a team efficient solution will be chosen. An accomplished football player must, together with adequate technique and specific mental and physical qualities, possess football intelligence, insight in the game, and recognize the ever-changing situation. He must be able to choose very quickly the most team efficient solution out of the many possible solutions. Talk about complexity! This is also why from a young age on, the tactical and technical development of players should go hand in hand. Also, the youth football development process must be a structured, on-going team tactical maturation process.

In football, the ball is played with the feet and this makes the team tactical teambuilding process even more complicated than in sports where the ball is played with the hands. In team handball, volleyball and basketball the degree of accuracy is much greater when playing the ball. These games are less unpredictable!

The unpredictability factor in football is a unique resistance in every match compared to other sports. This specific feature influences the game complexity and that makes it more difficult to play a good and efficient match. Another feature is that football is a 'physical contact sport'. Volleyball is, because of lack of physical contact, less complex. The direct confrontation between players does not exist. Both teams have the use over their own half of the court, divided by a net. It becomes therefore easier for a coach to develop set patterns. This does not mean that volleyball and other sports do not have their own characteristics, and therefore possess their own difficulties. The complexity and the element of unpredictability are simply not as predominant. What about ice hockey? It is a sport where players constantly battle to control the puck in a very limited space, therefore there are continuous fast transitions in attacking and defending. Nevertheless, this sport is also not as complex as football. 5v5 is less complicated than 11v11. Furthermore, the composition of the team can be changed because there are plenty of stoppages of play. Often a team has to play with less than 5 players because of the constant sending off of players to the penalty box. Hockey does have its own difficulties; for example, the lighting speed of actions and movements.

Another feature is the length of the match. A football match lasts in theory 2x45 minutes. The intention of the rules allows for as few stoppages as possible and to benefit the continuous flow of the game. During the most popular sports in the USA, such as American football and baseball, there is always the matter of building up to a brief exciting moment. After which there is always plenty of time for relaxation and an intermission.

I have drawn attention to the differences in characteristics between several sports to show that the team tactical factors of football are complicated and difficult. The coach of a football team cannot, except during set-plays, rehearse tailor-made solutions. He can only 'design' a set of team tactical guidelines. The players will have to come up with the correct solutions on the field. The guidelines give direction to increase the performance level. To train adequately is therefore vital, team spirit being the most important element.

THE COMPLEXITY OF FOOTBALL IS DETERMINED BY:

▶ the size of the team;
▶ the individual qualities combined with versatility;
▶ out of several options every player must quickly make the most team efficient choice ;
▶ the ball is played with the feet (accuracy);
▶ physical contact;

- ▶ the duration of the match;
- ▶ the measurements of the field;
- ▶ team tactically it is a players - and not a coaches game, given the degree of unpredictability;
- ▶ the constant action.

Conclusion: the game of football is team tactically an extremely difficult sport.

Necessity: a set of team tactical guidelines, which form a framework.

LIMITS OF TEAM BUILDING

At all levels, every coach will make an effort to improve his team's performance. He will make an attempt to reach this goal by helping to develop an extra team tactical dimension in every player based on the individual capacities of each player. Every player has to be able to perform his specific role in a team efficient manner. Being team efficient means: 'to create as many possible chances to score, and to give up as few chances as possible'. This will give ground to success.

I do not say deliberately: 'team efficient solutions will guarantee success'. To score and get scored on depends to a large degree on the individual quality of each player. A chance to score can be created through excellent teamwork. The actual finishing touch when scoring a goal is done specifically by one individual. Good combination play implies good teamwork, but it is not a guarantee for a positive result. For that to occur, the team needs players who have the ability to score, strong defenders and a competent goalkeeper.

This is one of the limitations a coach has to deal with while striving to increase the performance level of his team. There are more limits. These limits are determined by several essential factors with endless variations. A few of which I will mention:

QUALITY OF THE PLAYERS

The most important factor is the quality of the players. What does each player contribute: physically, mentally, technically, but especially tactically? The insight of how to resolve situations during the match determines to what extent the physical, mental, and technical qualities can be put to use.

BALANCE

Another determining factor is the capability of the coach and his players to find the right balance between defending, building-up, and attacking. Players must be competent in performing their role in their specific position, in their function as a defender, midfielder or attacker. To find the right balance is one of the most difficult assignments of a coach because it is not often possible to put the ideal line-up on the field.

SUCCESS

Success is a powerful weapon in the team building process. It gives the coach instant credibility concerning his coaching abilities, and it gives the players motivation as team players.

OPPONENT

Also the opponent influences the limits of the performance level of the team. You can play as well as the opponent permits you to and the other way around. Tactical countermeasures can undermine the performance level. What works today might not work at all next week.

UNPREDICTABILITY

Another factor is that the 'unpredictable' course of the match can have a positive, but also a negative impact on the performance of the team. Suddenly the keeper or a defender blunders. A red card is given to a player who could not control his temper. Or a different player can not handle the intimidation by his opponent. In another game, a questionable decision by the referee, the influence of the crowd, or a lack of luck decides the course of the match. If in 1978, during the World Cup in Argentina, a shot by Rensenbrink in the final minute of the game would have gone two centimeters to the right, instead of hitting the post, the Netherlands would have been crowned World Champion.

A very good example of the unpredictability of a match is the Champions League final of 1999 between Manchester United and Bayern Munich. After 60 minutes of play nobody doubted that Bayern would win the match 1-0. Manchester United took risks to try and win the match, and neglected their basic defensive tasks. This gave some great chances to the German team who would have decided the match with another goal. But,... two set plays during injury time were enough to guarantee an exciting and unpredictable change in the course of the match. A result that even the most knowledgeable person a few minutes earlier would not have thought possible. The eventual win of Manchester United proved again that a coach needs to be lucky at the right moment. Even if you have prepared your team well, and even if you have played well, every coach needs luck.

Every match contains moments, which have a positive influence on the performance of one coach's team and a negative influence on the team of the other coach. It happens most often in game situations

in which one or more players, in a split second, fail to act in a team efficient manner and disturb the team cohesiveness. In each European or
World Championship there are examples to give in which one moment
of 'mental weakness' from one player decided the course of the match.
At the top level the opponent will immediately profit from this mistake!

It is this element of unpredictability that keeps spectators glued
to their seats. Most of the time it is possible to keep this human failure
from happening in a well oiled football machine, but total security is not
possible. Thank goodness!

SOME FACTORS THAT DECIDE THE LIMITS OF
TEAM TACTICAL TEAM BUILDING:

▶   individual qualities of the complete group of players ;
▶   the balance in the team;
▶   level of success;
▶   tactical counter measures of the opponent;
▶   the unpredictability factor during the course of a match.

EXTERNAL FACTORS WITH REGARD TO THE
PSYCHOLOGICAL TEAM BUILDING PROCESS

The performance level is never a constant factor. It is always subject to
undermining or positive influences. Usually these are external factors.
For example, the tranquility or unrest within a club, or the influence of
the media can have an impact on the team spirit or on the willingness of
the player to devote his qualities to reach a common goal. One rotten
apple can spoil the bunch. This contaminating element is often the star
player, who is also the fan and media darling. We sometimes refer to
these players as a nail in the coach's coffin. This mental willingness to
function as a team player under all circumstances is not a natural
human behavior. There is always tension between self-interest and the
interest of the team. This is not only true in the football world.

POWER STRUGGLE

At Feyenoord, Rotterdam the performances suffered for years because
of a power struggle between board members. The club only became
successful when the professional staff gained more authority and started to work on creating the correct team mentality, and from there
worked on the team tactical development. If the team mentality is not
up to par you will not be able to develop team tactics. The misuse of
power within an association, a club, and also in the corporate world will
always negatively influence the performance level and therefore the
result.

The ongoing conflict at Ajax, Amsterdam about the transfer of Ronald and Frank de Boer to FC Barcelona had a negative impact on the performance level of the team during the 1998-1999 season. During the World Cup of 1990 and the European Championships of 1996, a rift in the team caused the performances to be down.

During a power struggle, and if power is misused, in whatever form, self-interest prevails over the interests of the team. Because the 'actors' cannot or will not see this, we cannot get rid of this phenomenon and ...This is not only true in athletics!

STATEMENTS

Statements made by a board member, a coach or a player, interpreted rightly or wrongly, can create a rift or cliques in a group. It is pure poison for the team spirit and also for the performance level.
The coach must therefore always be on the look-out. He should always focus on the very complex team building process. He is never finished with that. A good coach is a magician. Only he possesses the ingredients, the instruments to work magic and pull a top-level performance out of a hat. There is no one who can assist him with that task. Only the coach knows the tricks needed to reach his goal: to let every player function optimally with devotion to his teammates, without losing track of his own identity and personality, his own interpretation and insight into the game.

This is a very complicated task, trying to convince star players that they first of all should play in a team efficient manner at the service of the other 'stars'. This places a high demand on the credibility of the coach, which he gained through his qualities, good name and fame as a football player and coach, and his capability to transfer his insights and football vision to others.

Especially at the top, a clear football vision is a must. Every coach has to be convinced of his own vision and he has to have confidence in himself. Otherwise he will have a hard time trying to indoctrinate others and getting his message across. His vision must be football realistic: the ideas have to be devoted to the success, winning.

There are relatively few experts in top football who are able to influence the performance level in a positive manner. It is not the big picture that is important, it is all about the very specific team tactical details. These details must make top players with their special qualities perform just a little better within the team. Naturally, not even a good coach can start anything without a competent administrative, managerial, and football technical staff. Especially at the football technical department, we notice more and more specialists. Developmental directors, scouting experts, specific youth coaches and youth team administrators, youth football coordinators, keeper trainers, technical directors... But also specialists in fitness training, food science, and academic counselors. All of them are supporting the 'football magicians', the great helmsmen.

Only they are responsible for the performance. They are the only ones who will be held accountable. There is no other way. Although they will need to have control over everything. For as long as they are in charge, all the other staff members will need to support them unconditionally, from top to bottom. There can only be one goal: 'to do what's best for the team'. Unfortunately, there are an indefinite number of mantraps and snares. But that is also part of the game. In athletics, emotions and sentiments are often stronger than common sense.

LEVELS OF DEVELOPMENT

ALL LEVELS

It is a challenge for coaches at all levels to make players perform better. In the top of youth and amateur football, and in the professional leagues, the need exists for both coaches and players to reach the optimal performance level. The differences in quality are anchored in the big difference that exists between the potential of all the individuals within the talent pool. It is all about reaching the limits of the performance level of your team.

Team building is as old as the game of football itself. Coaches at all levels worked and still work on the team building process. But, I stress again that in modern day football, team building has to be seen as a total process, which is handled methodically. This demands that the coach, besides technical knowledge (as a player), possesses well-developed theoretical knowledge both of the game of football and the team building process. He also must have the ability to transfer his knowledge to others.

The team building process requires, just as the individual development does, from a young age on, a structural approach to it's development. This was not an issue in the era when all the kids played football day in and day out on small pitches on the street. You learned to know the ropes from playing on the streets. From the age of twelve on, a coach, who was usually a former player at a football club, took care of the remainder that had to be learned. After the disappearance of the 'street football education', so called experts looked for solutions to compensate for the big drop in both playing time and playing space. This development is still continuing at the present time. This is caused by the complexity of the matter.

Next to football technical aspects, political, organizational and economical aspects influence the matter. There is still a big diversity of

opinions when it comes to the football technical aspects of the game. It is still true that 'whoever wins, is correct'. For the real authorities on youth football, there are enough facts about football technical aspects to link the ideas together. An important prerequisite to accomplish this is to realize that it is more important to solve problems within youth football than to argue over who has the right ideas.
We will not even start to discuss the other aspects...

Too often people just do whatever they wish. They are just keeping the adults and youth players occupied, instead of methodically teaching them how to play the game based on well developed ideas. The youth players should most of all enjoy the football activities that are organized for them. The more professional the match, the more the real enjoyment will take a back seat. Playing football as a hobby and as a profession will melt together.

It is essential that over and over again the football world has to understand that important choices have to be made. This is especially true because of the drastic drop in 'training' time through the disappearance of 'street football'. The couple of hours a week spent training at a football club have now become very precious. These training sessions have to be organized very efficiently, with the starting point being training football realistic situations. In chapter 5, which deals with the football learning process for all age groups, I will go over this in more depth with the support of football technical facts.

WORLD CLASS LEVEL

To make the relationship clear between team building and the performance level, I will now go with more depth into the preparations of the Brazilian team who won the World Cup in 1994, which was held in the USA. For over two years the Brazilian coach Carlos Parreira was working on the team building process to create a solid team out of eleven individual first-rate players. He used Mario Zagallo, who won the World Cup with Brazil in 1970, as his advisor.

After 1970, Brazil had won no more World Cups, although they were the favorite to win every championship between 1974-1990 based on their talented group of players.

In 1970, Brazil won the World Cup by using the then revolutionary 4:2:4 team organization. This system did not get a big following in the rest of the football world due to its defensive vulnerability and the high-quality players you need to have to play this kind of team-organization. Only Ajax-Amsterdam used this team organization as a variation to the 4:3:3 system. During the first match at the World Championship held in Spain in 1982, Brazil changed from a 4:3:3 to a 4:4:2 system. They stuck with that concept ever since!

At the world class level it became apparent that the 4:2:4, 4:3:3 or 3:4:3 systems were vulnerable defensively and sensitive to quality. This was painfully shown by the Netherlands during World Cup '94 in the USA and European Cup '96 in England. Even the 4:4:2 system of the Dutch team coached by Guus Hiddink during World Cup '98 was defensively a bit too vulnerable during the decisive matches. It is all about the details. Dutch football does not possess a strong culture in which excellent man-to-man defenders are developed. In the Dutch youth education, the emphasis lays on defenders who can defend an area and can help in the build-up. This is an attractive choice, which only takes them so far. At the real top-level the lack of excellent man-to-man defenders is a danger to the result of the match. This is the reason that most countries play in a 3:5:2 or a 4:4:2 organization with 'real' man-to-man coverage.

Back to Brazil. Also, Carlos Parreira chose during the preparation to World Cup '94 for the 4:4:2 system. From the start he linked a few essential team tactical basic rules to it. He demanded that the entire team had to defend while the other team had possession of the ball. This included forwards Romario and Bebeto. This was an especially tough assignment for Romario. When playing at PSV-Eindhoven he never helped in defense and when he did help he did not know how. Because of that, Romario caused a bigger threat for the result of the match than if he remained up front. During that period in his career his team tactical awareness was not very well developed, concerning both his attitude and his execution.

Another one of Parreira's guidelines was: to turn the ball over as few times as possible during the build-up. Thus there was no room for individual actions, which were not team efficient. This was in the beginning especially tough on the playmaker in the midfield. He was just a little too artistic and hung on to the ball too long. This Player did not play simple and efficient enough in relation to the interests of the team, and the result. For the real fans of the game the specific football qualities of such players give the game an extra dimension. These players are indispensable, for both teammates and coaches, if they efficiently put the extra quality they possess to use for the team. If this is not the case, the opponent will exploit the mistakes of these players. Both of these team tactical guidelines demand a perfect team spirit. The 'star' forwards and the playmaker are vulnerable in the strive to comply with these guidelines. This was not only true for the Brazilians, but they do have at their disposal the majority of the ball virtuosi. Parreira needed two years of intense preparations to overcome this vulnerability! That goes to show how difficult the team building process can be. Even the best players in the world need time to learn how to play in a team efficient manner! It is all too easy for this process to be in conflict with the real character of individual players...

What were the other important aspects of the team building process during this two-year period? The team was constantly reminded by Parreira of the fact that the Brazilian people had ever since 1970 been dreaming about winning another world championship. He stressed that only this team could fulfill this wish. Only they could give the nation a boost. In Brazil, a world title means that millions of people can forget the misery of their daily life and the poverty for a while. A world title gives instant self-confidence to the people of Brazil. Parreira consciously used the dream of the Brazilian people and the role of this group of players to let that dream come true as an adhesive. Striving for: unity and team spirit. This is not a goal in itself, but it forms the psychological foundation for the team tactical development.

To boost the tranquility and unity within the team, Parreira installed a few essential rules concerning behavior on and off the pitch. It is not a simple task to realize this indispensable tranquility around a Brazilian team where there is usually a lot of turmoil. Players were not allowed to speak about money or bonuses anymore. 'All the money in the world can not equal becoming 'World Champion for the good of the Brazilian people, and you are the only ones that can make this dream come true'.

In contrast to the past, no journalists, agents, friends or even family members were allowed to enter the training camp facilities. Parreira made it clear to the players that this was the only way to bond as a team.

Outside of the hotel where the team resided, a sort of social room was created where the team could be met. At times, which suited the schedule of the team, journalists could interview them, and family and friends could meet with their loved ones. This separate meeting room gave the coach the opportunity to control the situation and the team had only eyes for each other at the training facility. This is an indispensable necessity to start communicating with each other.

A business engineer, who had a lot of experience with the team building process in the business world, was added to the staff. He was successful in showing players how the team building process works by using actual practical experiences.

The scrimmages were especially helpful in bringing the team tactical guidelines to life. Not the result, but the execution is what counted. Especially in the beginning there were some poor results that received plenty of criticism. This time around, the criticism did not influence the team!

The 4:4:2 system of Brazil differs a lot from most other 4:4:2 organizational forms. The backs play an important role during the build-up. A central defender will cover the position of the back who got involved. The center of the defense is amongst others covered by the central midfield player. His task is to be a kind of sweeper in the midfield and he plays a key role in distributing short and long passes. He is the first playmaker. Midfield players who are focussed on the attack and players who have a more controlling task behind the attackers characterize the midfield line of the Brazilians. The team tactical guidelines Parreira gave to his attackers, when the team had possession of the ball, entailed a lot of movement and going deep. They were especially not allowed to play too close together in the center of the attack and they had to be able to receive the ball in the space on the flanks.

During the team building process it is all about using the available group of players to develop as optimally as possible the three team functions. Due to the transitions between possession and possession by the opponent it is obvious that finding balance between those three functions is difficult to establish. This can vary from game to game. Just think about the difference between playing at home or away, the possibility that the opponent is favored to win, special circumstances or the pressures from outside the team. This balance asks for fine-tuning. By varying the line-up the Brazilian players became familiar with this phenomenon over a two- year period.

In 1994, Parreira succeeded in convincing his team of the necessity of a good balance between the three team functions. Parreira received a lot of criticism about his strive to have his star players play as team efficient as possible during home games. While playing in Brazil, the public's eye is always focused on the moments when the Brazilian team is in possession of the ball. But, on the other hand, it delivered the Brazilian people another much desired world title, after having waited 24 years!

The thing Bernstein did with a top-notch orchestra, and an artist like Carreras, namely give an extra dimension to the total performance capacity, also happened when Parreira coached the Brazilian team. He received a little bit more and a little bit better than the class that these stars already possessed. Parreira realized that the mental aspect of team building demanded a very subtle approach, especially when it concerned a team loaded with 'stars'.

The unity of the Brazilian team was clear both before and after the match. As a symbol of their unity the players walked on the field holding hands, just like a living chain. After the final whistle blew the whole team stood together and celebrated the win for several minutes. This happened also after the championship match. All this spontaneously!

In 1994, a sophisticated team building process arranged for the success to happen. During the championship match in 1998, Brazil did not succeed in getting the optimal performance out of the team. The most important reason: they lacked confidence in each other and therefore in the team! It did not help that Ronaldo collapsed both mentally and physically. This time they lacked that little bit extra.

STEPS IN THE DEVELOPMENTAL PROCESS

This first chapter has shown that in modern football, there was a rapid development of team tactics. The necessity to win, or at least not to lose, can be blamed on this phenomenon. When the ball is lost no one can hide and not defend. No attacker can only rely on his specialty, attacking. In modern football, the same motto has applied for years: eleven players participate during the defense and eleven players participate during build-up and attack. Not only by having a lightning fast transition from one team function to the next one, but especially by acting in the most team efficient manner.

During the period that Anderson was a striker for FC Barcelona, he complained to the press that he had to do so much defensively that he lacked the strength to attack. In his opinion, that was the reason why he did not score many goals. By making this remark, he showed that he was not brought up in the era of modern football. He did not meet the high standards that are demanded of top-level players. Just think about the workload of the forwards of Italian club Juventus when they were coached by Lippi, and dictated the European football scene. These forwards were not only very dangerous when in possession of the ball, but for the whole 90 minutes they had a quick transition when the ball was lost. Due to their team tactical insight, they did not do any unnecessary running.

Only in a very cohesive team is it possible for a well-trained athlete to perform efficiently. To run aimlessly wears you out. This was Anderson's problem at Barcelona.

Developments in football over the years have contributed to the fact that the easiest part, defending, has been perfected team tactically in every position. Through applying defensive pressure over the whole field, the team in possession gets little time and space to act and react. Due to this, a lot of improvements can be made both in the build-up and in the attack. Every player must, next to perfecting his individual qualities, profit from acting in a team efficient manner. This adds an extra dimension and difficulty factor to the game. It is imperative that the coach has mastered the subject and has a lot of credibility with the team.

Good coaching, to improve individual qualities, already demands a lot of know-how from the coach about the game. It is even harder to improve the team tactical qualities of all the players. It is not enough for a coach to just rely on his experiences as a player. More is needed. Team tactical coaching demands that the coach is able to break down and analyze the match in team tactical components. In other words, how the 'football orchestra' operates harmonically in defense, during the build-up and in the attack. You have to be able to 'read' the game; thus competently analyzing is a must. Where can the execution be improved, taking into account the individual and team tactical execution of the opponent? This demands, next to practical knowledge, a lot of football theoretical knowledge from the coach. A good coach will spend hours and hours analyzing the team tactical aspect of matches, both during the match and later while using video recordings. The knowledge he has gained will project on his team. Where are we failing as a team, as a line or as a functional group? For example, the cooperation between players in the center of the field, or between the left defender and the left midfield player etc., etc. This is a very time consuming assignment. And still, each player can increase his value to the team by increasing his insight. By going one meter forward or back, to the inside or to the outside, by a little bit more anticipation, by receiving the ball a little simpler.

And then you still have not completed your job as a coach. The hardest part is yet to come! Which training exercises should I choose to work on the shortcomings? How can I perfect the team tactical guidelines and thus the tactical variations? In other words: how can I make my training as meaningful as possible? This demands a lot of insight in training from the coach. He must recognize the team tactical aspect, analyze it, make it trainable in an exercise that makes that team tactical aspect come to life.

Most coaches do not reach the final step. They do not reach further than creating general training exercises, which hardly have any relation to problems that occurred in the match. The match conditions are not being simulated. The individual tactical insight is developed, but the players, for example, do not learn to make the translation from the positional games played during practice to the reality of the match. In a separate chapter (6) I present training sessions in which the team tactical simulation of the match is being realized as optimally as possible.

When analyzing the modern developments in football, you will have to conclude that during training sessions it is imperative to practice team tactical positional games to be able to improve the performance level. Team efficient speed of action does not rely only on the class of the individual, but also on efficient positioning of teammates. When the group gets the hang of these positional games during practice, then you are also working on an important aspect of mental team building. These kinds of team tactical assignments are the glue for team spirit and teamwork.

Football players usually lack the professional attitude to work on team tactical components. Nevertheless, this is a dire necessity. A coach who can get this across to his players proves his class more than ever! He must coax his players so they will make the team tactical aspects he has presented to them their own. Plenty of persuasion is needed to accomplish this.

For decades, coaches have accepted the lack of having a game mentality by players during training sessions. A lot of coaches currently are of a different opinion. More and more they have focused on the contents and intensity of the training sessions. This also means that players need to display a mentality during the positional games that approaches the mentality and team spirit needed during matches. Louis van Gaal, former coach of Ajax-Amsterdam and FC Barcelona and currently the coach of the Dutch national team was the big trendsetter, together with Marcello Lippi from Juventus. They demand this game mentality from their players during all training activities.

Naturally van Gaal and Lippi have the best players in the world at their disposal. I can hear you say: 'Well, if I had the best players, I could do it too' ... But it is difficult, especially with such a large group of top-notch players (about 20!), to mold them into becoming team players. In addition, the team has to show its superiority in every match they play. The internal and external pressure on the team is unbelievably immense. Success can only then be achieved when the team building process, both psychologically and team tactically, are mastered to the minutest detail. Only the very best coaches can succeed in this over a period of years. Naturally, the team building process at other levels is also a challenging job, but the pressure is less than at the absolute top level.

Marcello Lippi, the former coach of Juventus and currently at Inter Milan is part of a group of coaches who structurally work on the tactical team building process. That this process strains players is shown by the fact that even he, after having a few 'super-seasons', lost control over his team at Juventus. A new face, a new policy is then required.

The first success of teambuilding (1966)

Atmosphere is important for creating a feeling of togetherness (1967)

At the end of this first chapter I would like to mention that because of my ample experience in top-level football, I am convinced that coaches can profit from the guidelines for team building in the form of some kind of 'catalogue' in which they can look up certain aspects, depending on their needs, thus being a frame of reference when regularly working on improving the performance level. Team tactical maturity and willingness play an essential role in this frame of reference. In chapters 3 and 4 I will present such a frame of reference.

PERFORMANCE LEVEL

The building blocks for the most reachable performance level are:

The individual qualities of the players within your team:
▶ as much as possible in compliance with the team structure and style of play;
▶ sufficiently balanced in game mentality/qualities;
▶ excellent training qualities;
▶ Well-developed team building qualities (mental and team tactical).

The most negative influences on this are:
▶ the loss of key players;
▶ lack of success;
▶ negative audience;
▶ too many changes in trainers;
▶ lack of flexibility in relation to a realistic style of play;
▶ the negative internal and external factors in relation to the team building process and work environment;
▶ budget problems at the club;
▶ lack of having a right coach at the right place;
▶ having reached the top, lack of challenges;
▶ the youth education does not have center stage;
▶ overestimating and underestimating the opponent.

CHAPTER 2

THE EVOLUTION
OF THE GAME OF SOCCER

INTRODUCTION

The complexity of the game of soccer itself is lately being emphasized because of the evolution of the game. In 1974, the year in which the Dutch 'Total soccer' - pressuring the opponent on their own half with the purpose to win the ball back as soon as possible, was still an unknown strategy. This Dutch strategy received much praise from all over the world during the World Championship. Meanwhile, pressure football has become a much applied team tactical strategy. You try to give the opponent as little time and space as possible during their build-up. The modern day pressure football demands team tactical maturity from all players, no exceptions allowed!

Team defending has gone through an enormous development over the past 10 years. Each player has his own task to make it work, the forwards included. Pressure football is carried out by 11 players. The defensive block of 10 players can be shifted forward or backward, depending on the choices made by the coach.

The aim of playing pressure football on the opponent's half of the field is to: disturb and interrupt the build-up as early as possible, force them to deliver an inaccurate long ball to no one in particular, force them to play a square ball to gain time in which the lines can get organized again, or regain possession of the ball on the opponent's half of the field, followed by a quick transition.

The 'total' pressure style of football, especially well developed in England, puts the player with the ball under pressure. He has little time and space to act. More than ever, combination play, and thus high quality positional play, is a must. Furthermore, and lets not forget this, the individual qualities to be able to take in the correct position at the correct time, give a pass to put someone in a position to score, to cre-ate a chance and score the goal, is also a must. And,... do not hold on to the ball unnecessarily long. This last behavior is a persistent fault during the build-up. Make one step too many and the effect of a teammate who was available to receive the ball has disappeared. In particular, players who are good with the ball and enjoy having the ball make this mistake. They are convinced that they are doing a good job. These players can be especially important for the team concerning coming up with the best team efficient solutions on the field.

The evolution of the game of football is the most important reason why the team tactical development of the players should receive so much attention. This is why even higher demands are put on the individual qualities of players. Team tactical aspects and individual skills must be taught as early as possible during the youth football years of players. This demands high quality coaches and a perfected structure at the clubs and the youth educational system. World wide, much can be improved in this area! But it is a tough process, not only because of football related factors, but also, as mentioned earlier, due to political, economical, commercial and psychological factors.

To play a game of football just for fun is simple. The basic organization consists of: two goals (these could be made by jackets), a ball, two teams, a pitch and a few rules. That's all you need.

It gets more complicated when playing a league match. The coaches have to come up with ideas to improve the level of performance, for the individual as well as for the team. The key factor is to make it as hard as possible for the opponents. Not the game itself, but the result takes center stage!

Even more class and teamwork is demanded when you are not allowed to lose a league match because of the commercial interests involved. First of all, each coach has to have the class to develop his personal style of play, which because of the correct balance between defending, building-up and attacking leads to good results. It does not matter which team structure is chosen (the general team building process). This balance has to be a ready-made style of play for use in a competition match. While performing the style of play, it may be necessary to make tactical changes to adapt to the style of play and the performance level of the opponent (the specific tactical team building process). Even during the match it may be necessary to tweak the team tactics a little. However, these changes in team tactics should already have been developed! Sometimes you must utilize a totally different style of play. All of this entails a lot of training work and tactical talk sessions under the guidance of a skilled coach who has mastered this matter, both theoretically and practically. Much expertise is asked from the coach when it comes to training the team tactical 'fragments'.

And still, this is not a guarantee for consistent success. As a coach, you do have the security that you got everything possible out of your team. Nevertheless, there are no real limits to the maximum performance level. For that, coaches are too dependent on other factors such as the class of the key players, the working and living climate within the club, and even lady luck herself. However, a matured team tactical unit will ensure more tranquility, more confidence, and more stamina!

Cable channel Eurosport broadcasts regularly legendary football matches from the past. The difference is unbelievable compared to the matches played nowadays! It is so apparent that the players had much more time and space in duels, consequently the speed of action needed was much lower. Today, even absolute world-class players like Johan Cruijff and Franz Beckenbauer would have to utilize their extra qualities in a different way to be able to play with enough team efficiency. The transition from defending to attacking and vise versa takes place much quicker. The speed of action needed is many times faster, with the individual technical and tactical qualities as the basis. Due to better-developed concentration, players can better anticipate the game situations. The speed of play has increased quite a bit. The one-touch combinations are part of the ultimate art of positional play.

Furthermore, it is of vital importance to a team that a player who can make his mark on the speed of the match guides the build-up. This could be by one-touch, but also by consciously slowing down the speed of the match to give teammates time to get in the correct position. Players who can set the pace of the match are the diamonds of the team. However, they can not afford to be the odd man out concerning the defensive team function. This is their vulnerable side. Examples of such diamonds are; Guardiola (FC Barcelona), Litmanen during his stint at Ajax-Amsterdam, Hagi (Romania), van Gastel (Feyenoord-Rotterdam) and of course the star player of the World Championship of '98, Zidane (Juventus and the French national team). Almost every top team has this type of player at its disposal, although there are differences in the level of quality. How well he is able to function under a great deal of defensive pressure determines the difference in quality. In fact you can find this type of a player in every team at all levels, even in youth and amateur teams, but only a select few are good enough to reach the top.

It has become more difficult to create chances against increasingly better organized defenses. This is understandable because it is easier from a team tactical point of view to defend and adjust to the opponent than to build-up and attack yourself. This is why there is more room by the latter two team functions to improve the performance level.

The individual qualities of your players create the most important conditions, but do not guarantee an optimal team performance. To accomplish this, it is imperative to have a good coach, one who has been tried and tested by the practical and theoretical side of competitive football, and uses the modern team building mechanism as an important instrument.

The team building process may never be allowed to take away from the specific qualities of a player, thus not from his creativity, his artistic qualities and style of play. It is always the individual class, the individual way of experiencing the game, and the individual failing that seems to be the decisive factor in the utilization, implementation and interpretation of the team rules.

Only the player can anticipate the unpredictability of the constantly changing moments in the game. His team tactical education is focused on finding the most team efficient solution in every situation he comes across. This means: to get everything and maybe even a little more out of the game!

Not only does every player want to outsmart his opponent and win the 'battles', but he also wants to win the game! He can not do this by himself. He can only succeed with teamwork while defending, building-up and attacking. The individual challenge and team spirit are uncompromisingly linked together. It does not matter how many years they have played, how much money they have already made, the challenge and love for the 'battle' will never cease to exist even in top-notch players. This established fact forms the most important foundation for the coach to improve the performance level of the team.

Within this framework it will be obvious that the 'friendly' matches (a fake battle) more and more lack the challenge. These matches have their purpose in trying out different team tactical elements, but players will lack the utmost will to win and to explore new horizons.

TOP-NOTCH COACHES

The already mentioned evolution of the game of football can be attributed to, in the past decade, the influence of a few top-notch coaches. These coaches developed team tactical innovations, which improved the performance level of their teams. This was not a natural process. Due to the success of these coaches, other coaches also plunged into these new styles of play.

MARIO ZAGALLO (ATTACKING STYLE OF PLAY)

From the end of the 1950's, Brazilian football, due to its style of play, had a big influence on the European football scene. During the 1970 World Championship in Mexico, the main focus in the surprising 4:2:4-system was on the building-up and attacking functions. This contrasted sharply with the system used by the opponent in the final game, Italy. They choose to use the catenaccio concept of Helenio Herrera.

The Brazilian coach Zagallo defensively decided to use the covering of space and each player had to participate in defense. This makes good sense, because otherwise you would not be able to be successful with such an attacking style of play, including the types of players connected to that style. It was at that time that I watched absolute world-class players like Pelé, Tosao, Rivelinho and Jairzinho fall back on their own half after possession was lost!

Besides the Netherlands, not many other countries imitated the Brazilian style of play. There are several demonstrable causes for this. Attacking football is riskier and it demands top-notch players in every line. It also demands players who are used to it and have been brought up in this style of play. Most countries lack this kind of a football culture. It is also true that coaches do not get enough space to experiment with different styles of play. A style of play at the top must be realistic in yielding success. It is not a product of idealism!

HELENIO HERRERA (DEFENSIVE STYLE OF PLAY)

In contrast to the Brazilian style of play, the Italian style catenaccio resulted in the typical counter style football. They used a libero who played constantly behind the 4-man defensive line. They played man-to-man marking in the midfield and in the defensive line and that made it look like couples-football.

Partly due to the outstanding individual players at Inter Milan, Helenio Herrera achieved a lot of success in the sixties with this style of play. Brazil won the World Championship with a contrasting style of play - make the play, instead of gambling on the counterattack. This is the proof that success is always possible if you are able to link the individual qualities within the team to team tactical guidelines.

This does not alter the fact that the Brazilian style of play looks much more spectacular and risky than counter style football. Still, after the appealing success of the Brazilian team at the World Championship in Mexico, there are only a few countries who play an attacking style football! An attacking style is more difficult to develop. It places great demands on the insight in football from the players and their team tactical capacity. Counter style football uses a more wait-and-see approach and is more reactive. You try to profit from mistakes the opponents make in their build-up. This style is easier to carry out in respect to individual tactical and team tactical aspects; in other words it is easier to play. It is less vulnerable, and because of that, also more successful. An attacking style of play requires players who grew up playing this style of football as youth players. This is not as necessary when playing counter style football.

SIR ALF RAMSEY (THE DEMISE OF THE WING FORWARDS)

In the sixties, Sir Alf Ramsey made his mark on the English style of play. Until that moment, coaches in England automatically chose to use real wing forwards. In the preparation to the World Championship of 1966, Sir Alf Ramsey replaced the classical wing players with midfield players who had a more attacking task. Due to their capture of the world title in 1966, his choice gained a big following and the foundation was laid for the 4:4:2 system.

RINUS MICHELS (TOTAL - AND PRESSURE FOOTBALL)

In the seventies, I was known for utilizing two building-up/attacking strategies, which made their mark on the evolution of the game of football:
▶	the so called 'Total football' (Ajax-Amsterdam 1970)
▶	the attacking pressure football, the 'hunt' for the ball (World Cup 1974)

4:3:3 was the basic organizational form, from which I often chose to play the tactical variation 4:2:4. An extra forward would take the place of the attacking midfield player.

'Total football' was the consequence of my search for a way to break open the enforced defenses. This required actions during the build-up and attack that would surprise the opponent. This is the reason that I chose to have frequent changes in the positions, within and between the three lines. All players were allowed to participate in the build-up and attack as long as they also felt responsible for their defensive tasks. Individually and team tactically, this does put high demands on the players.

The main aim of the attacking pressure football, the 'hunt', was: regaining possession as soon as possible after the ball was lost on the opponents half during an attack. The 'trapping' of the opponents on their own half is only then possible when all the lines are pushed up and play close together. This automatically means that you give away a lot of space on your own half and you are vulnerable for counter-attacks.

This style of pressure football was actually a continuation, a variation of the 'Total football'. The aim was, after all, to also break open the enforced defenses through regaining possession on their half, and then right away change over to the attack according to the rules of 'Total football'.

'Total football' and its attacking pressure are very spectacular. It places great demands on individual and team tactical excellence. Such a development demands years of selecting players... and structural team building!

In 1974 and 1988, The Netherlands had these essential excellent players at their disposal. After a spectacular advancement on the international football scene, The Netherlands just failed to be the champion in World Cup '74 in and against Germany. In 1988, we won the European Championship, which was also held in Germany.

In the preparations to that Championship, we trained intensively on the strategical aspect in the build-up, namely the timing of the deep pass; a team tactical training in which we focused on one detail of the team function. An absolute prerequisite, to master such a team tactical aspect, is that all the players possess a positive mentality, including the substitutes. It is a collective assignment. When the coach can convince the players of the need of this assignment, then the team tactical assignment also becomes an excellent bonding mechanism concerning the team spirit.

This same exact group of players, having matured over the 2 years, failed miserably during the World Championship of 1990, in Italy. I could fill a book writing about the causes of their failure... The underlying reason had to do with a failing team spirit.

FRANZ BECKENBAUER (5:3:2)

Due to the successes of Germany under the guidance of Franz Beckenbauer in the 1990's, a new organizational form made an entry: the 5:3:2 (defensive variation) or the 3:5:2 (building-up variation).

New in this concept were the two man-to-man-markers in the center with a sweeper who played defensively behind them and offensively in front of them. Another innovation was the defender on the outside who also had a job in the build-up. He had to cover the whole area on the outside from end line to end line. Most teams at the top international level choose to play this style created by Beckenbauer. Tactically there are several variations possible in the execution of the build-up and attacking strategies.

JOHAN CRUIJFF (3:4:3)

After my departure at Ajax-Amsterdam, Johan Cruijff was the first coach who continued to have a substantial influence on the further-development of the style of play. He reduced the 4-man defensive line to a 3-man line and played a more and more attacking style football, first with Ajax-Amsterdam and later on also with Barcelona. The main strategical innovation was to play with an extra midfield player at the expense of the back line. The aim was to control the midfield and strengthen the building-up team function.

He put up with the risks connected to this decision. The success of this system (3:4:3-formation) is dependant upon the individual excellence that serves this spectacular but risky style of play. It is a choice only a few coaches have made. This style places high demands on the tactical cohesiveness of the players in the center of the field. It demands that the players in those positions have a high level of football intelligence. There are hardly any followers of this style of play. This is the reason why I look at it as a variation on the 4:3:3-system.

LOUIS VAN GAAL (FURTHER DEVELOPMENT 3:4:3)

Louis van Gaal has further developed this style of play. Concerning the team tactical aspects, he works even more structurally than Johan Cruijff did. Van Gaal gives much attention to the team building process using a perfectly structured youth football education system as the foundation. Compared with 'Total football', there is less room in his approach for opportunism and changes in positions. On the other hand, the building-up team function is perfected to the smallest detail.

CHAPTER 3

THE GROUND RULES OF THE TEAM TACTICAL TEAM BUILDING PROCESS

INTRODUCTION

Top-level football finds itself in a transitional phase. A great deal has been achieved team tactically in defensive aspects, but a lot can still be improved in the build-up and attacking team functions. This is certainly the case when two teams with a different style of play face each other; for example, when a team from Great Britain plays against a team from the European mainland. For years British teams, because of their opportune style of play with its high speed, limited build-up strategies and therefore average positional play, had a tough time competing against other top European clubs. This was the reason that British top-clubs like Manchester United, Arsenal, Chelsea, Glasgow Rangers and Celtic had to change and adapt their style of play. To achieve this, coaches were hired from abroad who were experienced and well edu-cated in the team tactical aspects of the game. These coaches then strengthened their team by contracting the most suitable types of play-ers (some of them were foreign players). At this moment, this process is still continuing at a high rate. Only Manchester United has a British coach (Alex Ferguson) who takes part in this development process.

It is complicated to change to a different style of play. It asks much of players who have gone through an extended football education since they began playing at a young age. The Dutch playing style places different demands on its players than in any other football coun-try in the world. To play with only three defenders, you need to have both excellent man-to-man markers and players who are dominant in covering space, and who complement each other well. Also, the schooling of specific wing forwards asks for an investment of many years during the youth training period.

There are of course top-notch players who can, due to their outstanding qualities, function in any system. These are the exceptions to the rule. This does not stop me from stressing the value of a well functioning youth educational system to facilitate the development of a specific style of play for the first team.

THE BUILDING BLOCKS OF THE TEAM BUILDING PROCESS (MECHANISM)

▸ A continuing positive mentality to bring and keep the team tactical performance level up to standard.

▸ A coach who receives total support from the club management (administrators and training staff) while possessing credibility and a vision to bring the team   tactical mechanism, as most important 'team work instrument', to life.

▸ The most optimal individual performance level, suitable to solve the ever changing game situations individually and team tactically in a positive way.

▸ The style of play, constructed out of tactical organizational, general tactical and specific tactical guidelines with the aim to reach the optimal performance level.

▸ Training activities, focussed on the functional technical development while taking in account the different age groups.

▸ Training activities which link the functional technical development to team tactical development.

▸ The tactical global match performance level is the standard, in the total composition of performance pyramids.

▸ The challenge of the game, the desire to be the better team, the desire to win, as the common goal of the youth educational system.

▸ The ever increasing pressure to succeed at the top level as the inevitable stimulus.

▸ Modern schooled team tactical coaching qualities.

▸ Team tactical coaching maturity of the key player

TOOL

The team building process is the tool the coach uses to develop the football concept, the style of play, as optimally as possible with the aim to achieve success. The football concept, also known as the match concept, is seen as the theoretical side of the team building process. The style of play is the implementation of the concept on the field. Through analyzing a football concept, several important elements can be described:

- The team organization;
- Tasks and functions within this team organization;
- the strategies within the three team functions
  (defensive, during the build-up and attacking);
- The tactical variations to the general style of play, to be able to adapt to typical difficulties faced within the match.

It is not a simple task to structure the team tactical team building process in guidelines that make sense, are useful and well organized. However, a coach can formulate ground rules which he can base his teamwork on.

I strongly believe that a coach has to stick to his principles within the team building process, even if there is a chance that the result of a match may not turn out in his favor. Players have a nose for coaches who doubt themselves. His credibility, his most important commodity, will get hurt. He can have doubts, but he can not show this. It might be a good idea to have a discussion with your key players, preferably to confirm your beliefs. Top-level players want to have a say in things, so it is a must to communicate with them. However, the hierarchy has to remain clear!

Tactical variations give the coach enough latitude. Nevertheless, it is crucial that his players possess enough qualities to be able to carry out the variations during the match.

YOUTH FOOTBALL PLAYERS

The methods used by a coach while working with youth players, concerning team building, are clearly different for as long as the development of individual players has the priority over the result of the matches. Until about 14 years of age, the team tactical development goes on without effort. After that it becomes more and more a conscience process. There are exceptions to the rule, but mostly this begins at about age 17-18.

After his youth football days are over, every player becomes part of an adult team where he has to learn that the result is the only thing that matters. From a mental point of view, this is a tough learning process. Only a selected few will gain a starting position. Most players mature while playing for the reserve team or sitting on the bench with the first team. Players of this age group absolutely need a strong coach of their own. A big disadvantage for this age group in the Netherlands is that there is no real league for them where they get tested every week. The league for the reserve teams of professional clubs does not fulfill the need.

Every youth player till the age of 18 must, as much as possible, get the opportunity to display his creative ways and therefore develop

his talents optimally. However, this freedom is bound by a set of guidelines. The team tactical guidelines also provide youth players something to fall back on, and to be able to win as a team. This can only
succeed during matches if the players possess the essential game
mentality.

TOP-NOTCH PLAYERS

For top-notch players, the general guidelines are not sufficient anymore.
The higher the level of play, the more important the interpretation
becomes of the team tactical details. Especially those details concerned with the positional and combination play. Just one meter to the
right or left, even better anticipation, even better timing, even better
communication, etc., etc. This in itself places higher demands on the
mentality and the willingness to improve the details. To improve a little
at the top demands the utmost in mental aspects; in particular, to be
receptive to the team building process.

It is a tough job to make the team tactical details clear to the
players. You must translate what has occurred in the match into training activities which are linked to these guidelines. This must be done in
such a way that they can be executed again in the matches. I call this
the simulation of the match reality during training sessions. There are
often training activities that keep the players busy, but when training is
over, the players cannot make the translation to the match reality. This
is a waste of time and energy. It is crucial to recognize in a match what
has been practiced in training! Top-notch players need to be able to
coach themselves during training and scrimmages if details need to be
improved.

WORKING IN A STRUCTURAL FASHION

Many coaches find it difficult to work in a structural fashion with their
team. They would much rather work on the basis of their intuition or
their experience as a player. In the past, that was mostly sufficient. In
chapters 1 and 2, I discussed the fact that top-level football has gone
through major developments. This evolution has far-reaching consequences for the demands put on the coach and his team. If you want to
remain at the top, then the coach must work structurally to improve
team tactical aspects. To be able to do this, the coach must possess
the theoretical knowledge of the football team building process.

I have translated the ground rules of the team tactical team
building process in a set of guidelines. These were taught at the most
advanced coaching course in the Netherlands. After passing this
course, coaches are licensed to coach at the professional level. These
guidelines can be broken down into the following:

- Organizational guidelines (from the tactical point of view);
- Strategical guidelines (general tactical);
- Tactical guidelines (specific tactical).

A coach can decide for himself what is of use to him. Coaches who are very experienced might only pick up a few new facets, because they have developed themselves already in dealing with the team building process. Young and inexperienced coaches who are still involved in coaching courses will find that this framework gives them a reference in their daily functioning.

ORGANIZATIONAL GUIDELINES   FORMATIONS

The main question for the first guideline is: in which organizational form does your team play or do you want your team to play in, taking the available group of players into account?

ORGANIZATIONAL FORMS

Three main organizational forms can be distinguished: 5:3:2, 4:4:2, 4:3:3. I am of the opinion that all other concepts are derived from these three! Within these three organizational forms several variations are possible, but at the kick-off you can always recognize one of the three basic organizational forms. In the execution of these forms, an abundance of variations are revealed, concerning the defense, the build-up, and the attack.

The 4:2:4- system as a style of play has almost disappeared. Brazil used it in 1970, and they won the World Championship. Also, Ajax-Amsterdam played this style in that period in history. It sadly disappeared due to its defensive vulnerability. At the international top-level, even the 3:4:3-system which was cherished for years by the Dutch national team coaches has shown to be too vulnerable.

For all these organizational forms, with their specific strategies during defending, building-up and attacking, the positional play must be as flexible as possible. Furthermore, during the match it must be possible to implement tactical variations, in case of being behind in the score or ahead, when playing an away or home game, or due to the qualities of the opponent. It is all about the specific tactic used in that match. This tactic remains based on the general concept of the game and when it is executed it is called the style of play.

During the match a coach can play with a balance between defending and attacking, within his steady style of play, and change the emphasis to one or the other. Also, the description of the task and function of one or more players can vary from game to game. It does not matter which organizational form you choose, but there needs to be a balance concerning the attacking, the build-up and the defensive forces, depending on the type of match.

Every system has its pros and cons. <u>It is all about minimizing the cons and taking advantage of the pros</u>. Everything is decided by the execution of the system and is therefore dependent upon the available pool of players. The way each player positively or negatively influences the result depends on how he performs his specific tasks within the framework of the tactical team rules. Therefore, the coach must have insight into the tasks of each player; the defensive tasks, the tasks during the build-up, and the attacking tasks, within the organizational form.

The coach chooses the organizational form. The discussion is still continuing about the basic assumption that 'the quality of the available player pool determines the team structure and the execution and not the other way around.' Practical experience shows that there is another way. The coach chooses which team structure he believes will give him the most success. He fits the players into this team structure. If necessary he will look for a new player to put in a position that needs to be occupied by a better player or he changes the positions of one or more players till he finds a match that fits both the players' qualities and himself. This final scenario occurs more often.

The coach decides on the team structure and team strategies. The 'ideal' performance can be achieved when using the available players in the most optimal way.

SOCCER HISTORY

In most countries, the football culture and history are important factors when determining which organizational form is chosen. The system of play of the national team is often repeated in the way the top clubs play. Since the success of Franz Beckenbauer in Germany, the national team has played a 5:3:2 or a 3:5:2 system. In my opinion, you cannot talk about two different team organizations within their style of play. The real question you should ask is if, in the defensive five-player line, both outside backs when considering their tasks and functions and therefore their qualities, should be considered midfield players or more as outside backs as seen in the Brazilian four-man line. These outside backs participate in the build-up and attack. On the basis of the types of players used and the applied defensive and build-up strategies, it seems that the 5:3:2 system is their basic structure.

Another good example of a football country where the national teams and clubs choose the same organizational form is England. They play a 4:4:2 with a flatback-four defensive line, just like the Brazilians, the Swedes, and the Norwegians. The Brazilians use a dif-

High and dry to oversee the team tactical details (1968)

The opponent can determine the tactical variation of the style of play (1969)

ferent tactical coherence between the midfield and the defenders when considering the transition when gaining possession. Also the 4:4:2 system has many variations in its execution due to the differences in the diverse strategies. You can speak of a recognizable team structure for all followers of the 4:4:2 system. However, the execution of the system can, depending upon the football vision of the trainer, luckily be sufficiently flexible. Once again the efficiency of the concept of the game can fail or succeed through the contribution of your players.

Another example is Italy. Most teams play a 4:4:2 system. The coaches then choose which variations within the system they desire. There are Italian teams who play with two real strikers, whereas other teams play with a deep striker and a support striker or an attacking midfielder behind him. Such variations can also be found in the placement of the players in the midfield. During the time period that Van Basten - Gullit - Rijkaard played at AC Milan, they had a four-man midfield in one line. Each player had his own specific task: one player more controlling/regulating and the other more supportive/attacking. Other Italian coaches choose to use two central midfield players and two 'free' outside midfielders. Such a choice is determined by your ideas as a coach about the preferred execution of the system and also by the available pool of players. Of course, it will always remain a 4:4:2 system, which is obvious during the kick-off.

I would like to come back to the 3:4:3 system. I do not see this as the fourth organizational form, because it is hardly used by anybody. At Barcelona, Van Gaal played with this system. This was an exception to the rule. You can also look at it as an attacking variation of the well known 4:3:3.

CLUB TRADITION

Besides the style of play of the national team, the tradition at the club can also play a role in which system is played. One of the clearest examples is the style played by Ajax-Amsterdam. For years and years they have played an attacking style football with two specific wing forwards. Coaches can modify the style of play just a little bit, however it will be unthinkable to have an Ajax team play counter football without the wing forwards. Even Ajax head coach Ivic came to find that out the hard way. To have success is not even important at that moment, because the fans hate the tactical choice. His conservative style of play based on 'counter football' and not on 'making the play' never had a chance within the Ajax-culture.

VISION OF THE COACH

When choosing a certain style of play, the vision of the coach also plays an essential role. Is it your goal as a trainer to have the best results, or is the level of entertainment also an issue? In most countries it is imperative that a coach 'just' wins. It is not important how he gets that done. The Netherlands football culture is unlike the others, and people are of a different opinion. Winning alone is not enough in The Netherlands. What counts is how you win. Dutch trainers have to realize that as the man in charge you might have to pay a price for this combination of result and entertainment value.

An example of this was the Dutch first division club MVV-Maastricht. During the 1990's they tried to play an attractive style of football and were even named 'Club of the Year' once. However, when the club started losing games during the '94-'95 season, and kept playing this risky style, they were unexpectedly relegated with disastrous consequences.

A style of play above all needs to be result realistic. Therefore, I state that for all teams, the result needs to be the focal point. To strive for success is an important element in the team building process. A style of play can be performed with the emphasis on defending or attacking. The coach has already taken this into account when he established the general or specific tactical guidelines. A lot depends on the quality of the players on his team, the expectations of the team in the competition, and the vision of the coach. Not the organizational form (system), but the general tactical guidelines describe if the emphasis is on playing on the counter attack (defensively oriented), or more on a play making style of football (offensively oriented). The reality of being successful has the main priority and it demands a certain level of flexibility in the guidelines for the defensive, build-up and attacking team functions. One 4:4:2, 5:3:2 or 4:3:3 is not necessarily like another!

ADVANTAGES AND DISADVANTAGES

The endless discussions about what organizational form is the best are actually unnecessary. The coach gets the best out of the chosen organizational form if he has done everything he can to influence the advantages positively and tries to minimize the disadvantages. The 'ideal' organizational form does not exist in regard to the result. With any system you can win and lose. It is all about the execution and the players who have to make the organizational form come to life on the field.

It is of course imperative that the coach knows the advantages and disadvantages of every organizational form and how to deal with them. Once more I state that every organizational form has its advan-

tages and disadvantages when implemented. A coach is constantly busy with that process. Besides that, the coach of the opponent is trying to take advantage of the negative sides of your organizational form. The efficient execution of the chosen organizational form will also be determined by the so called 'match resistances':
- the well thought out counter measures (tactics);
- the twelfth- man (difference in crowd at home or away games);
- the thirteenth-man (decisions made by the referees);
- the score-line (box score);
- the luck factor.

The experiences of football games have taught us that in a period of one or two minutes the complexity of the game can change drastically due to the unpredictability of these resistances. Thus this unpredictability factor is an important match resistance. It appeals, therefore, constantly to the adequate match mentality of the players.

If both teams, for example, play in a 4:4:2 system, then there is always one team who is favored to win due to their home advantage, their ranking, or the history of this confrontation. You will then notice that with the team which started the game as the underdog, one or more players will get the assignment to take away specific qualities of the opponent in the execution of the style of play. Mostly this concerns build-up and attacking qualities. To be able to make these adaptations, it has been calculated in that players might have to change positions. When down or ahead in the game the same thing often happens. Especially when falling behind, players have a tendency to not play their role within the team anymore. They try to force the play. Therefore, the organization within the team decreases. They mean well, but their actions usually have the opposite effect. To be disciplined when performing the tasks within the team is a basic quality. This phenomenon also occurs when a team is leading. They want to be noticed or they slack in their efforts. Many games have been lost unnecessarily due to this phenomenon. To go back in time during such a game is almost always futile. The solid team organization has been undermined. Therefore, possession is lost more often, and the opponent gets better as the game goes on.

This phenomenon belongs to the sphere of influence of the match-related resistances. In my playing years, we once lost a game because of this phenomenon, after being ahead 5-1 we still managed to lose 5-6. As a trainer at Ajax, we beat the mighty Benfica in Portugal 3-1 after having lost 3-1 at home... You never know what is going to happen. This unpredictability, the magical forces in the sport: they are what makes football so attractive.

I will now go over the advantages and disadvantages of the execution of the three basic organizational forms in more depth. This is not an easy task, due to the fact that the execution of the chosen concept depends on the qualities of the individual players. Basically it is all about how the players are positioned on the field and how many players play in defense, the build-up and the attack. If the basic assumption is that you have 10 field players, then you could have 3 players for each function. One player remains, and he could play in one of the 3 functions. Usually he is the fourth defender. Some coaches in the Netherlands have the preference of putting this player in the midfield (3:4:3). During the evolution of top-level football, coaches placed the accent on the defensive team function at the expense of the attacking team function. You then end up with 5:3:2, 3:5:2 and 4:4:2. The quality of the positional play decides how well the disadvantages of that choice can be dealt with.

In 4:3:3 and 3:4:3 the positioning of the players is easily distinguishable, taking the size of the field and the three team functions into account. The positional play with two forwards is much tougher, both when in possession and when the opponent has the ball. After all, there are more spaces to operate in. However, this does not have to be a problem as long as there is good positional play in accordance with a set of team tactical guidelines. Actually, this is true for all team structures and their variations. This proves again the importance of the team tactical aspects, generally as well as in detail. This is what the main theme of this book; the team building process, is all about.

ORGANIZATIONAL FORM 5:3:2

In the organizational form 5:3:2, it is clear that the emphasis lies on the defensive line with 5 players. The chance is pretty good that defensively you will be in good shape. The most important disadvantage will become clear when your team wins the ball while the opponent was attacking. The 5 players will be positioned in the width of the field, and that is too many to be able to get a rapid, well-organized and efficient build-up going.

To be able to minimize this disadvantage you need to have an excellent team, including forwards who are good at holding on to the ball and waiting for support to arrive. Other players must be capable of getting the ball to the forwards. This demands good positional play from the forwards in relation to each other, the midfield players and the defenders. Furthermore the outside defenders must possess a great deal of physical and building-up qualities to negate the disadvantages during the transition when possession is regained. The lack of quality of such players has for years been a disadvantage for the style of play of German teams, who chose to play 5:3:2. These outside backs do have the physical qualities to move forward, but they get into trouble after they get the ball. Thus these German defenders often look to play the ball to the most creative midfield player or play a long ball to the forwards. The chance of losing possession is magnified.

To stress again that all can be lost and gained through the execution and the qualities of the individual players, I will compare the German outside defenders to their colleagues from Brazil. When Brazil regains possession of the ball during an attack of their opponent, for years the build-up has been orchestrated according to a set pattern. An outside back gets involved in the build-up, a central defender covers his position and a central midfielder becomes a central defender.

This outside defender can therefore fully concentrate on his task in the build-up. The difference is, compared to his German colleague, that the Brazilian defender has the build-up qualities of a midfield player. This of course has been developed during his years as a youth player. This is the reason Brazilian outside defenders are so popular in Germany.

Naturally, the German coaches also try to minimize the disadvantages of their organizational form. There is a tendency to look for outside defenders needed in the 5:3:2 system who possess the build-up qualities, and this type of player is being developed in the youth educational programs. A different solution was seen at the European Championship of 1996 in England, where coach Berti Vogts consciously opted for a slower pace in the build-up to gain time to get better organized. The sweeper Sammer played a key role in achieving this.

ORGANIZATIONAL FORM 4:4:2

The advantage of the 4:4:2-system is that you have enough players at your disposal to execute the build-up and the defensive tasks. A disadvantage could be that - and I notice this often at Italian clubs - the two forwards are too far away and thus are too isolated. This is the reason that more and more you see one deep forward, who can hold the ball and can cover a lot of space both deep and to the wings, and one creative support striker. Famous support strikers, also known as attacking playmakers are for example Zidane at Juventus and Zola at Chelsea. They excel in receiving the ball, dribbling and passing. Naturally this is linked to plenty of insight into the game.

A different problem for the good execution of the 4:4:2-system in Italy (and elsewhere), is to find the right types of players for the outside midfield positions. Although not as much as in the 5:3:2-system, these players do have to cover a lot of ground during the match. These players must be multi-functional; they must possess the qualities to play their role in all three team functions at the top-level.
These outside midfielders must have the tactical willingness to not

unnecessarily move toward the center of the field. It is expected of their teammates that they get these players optimally involved in the game. This is an important strategic guideline. Also this Italian version of the 4:4:2 is based upon a lot of players in the back line, because one of the two outside midfielders must cover the space of a central defender. This midfielder must come back and to the center to do this.

The Italian forwards play an important role in the 4:4:2 as players who need to be available to receive the ball. They are used to taking on the 1:1 battles.

A great many teams have problems finding the right players for the positions on the outside of the field. Often times, they started as midfielders or backs, and now they have to be able to beat a man on the outside and deliver a good cross. These players are very hard to find. In the Netherlands, when the 4:3:3-system is chosen the true wing forwards need to learn to play their defensive role. For that matter, it is easier to teach this to the forward than to teach a midfielder or defender the tasks of an outside attacker. This is logical, because it is easier to develop a defensive quality than a build-up quality. A type of player such as Beckham of Manchester United is worth a ton of money. He is the perfect outside player and an outstanding midfielder. In the golden years of Ajax they had Finidi George, who was both a wing forward and a midfielder.

ORGANIZATIONAL FORM 4:3:3

When choosing to play the 4:3:3-system, you are assuming as a coach that you will carry the play as much as possible. Right away this shows how difficult this will be. How many coaches dare to make this decision? Not many any more, especially not outside of the Netherlands. You are planning on playing preferably on the opponents half of the field and will therefore defend far away from your own goal. This is the reason that the opponents have a lot of space to play dangerous counter-attacks. Therefore you cannot afford to lose possession during the build-up.

The big advantage is that you play close to the opponents' goal. If you are capable of disturbing their build-up, than you can keep them constantly under pressure. Another advantage is that because of the players on the outside, the whole width of the field is taken care of, also when possession is lost. In addition, a lot of operational space is created in the center of the field. To be able to play this system to its fullest, the players in the center need to be tactically competent.

Naturally, top-teams that also play systematically on the counter attack can develop pressure in the attack. They mostly do this when they are losing or when they play against an underdog that keep a lot of players behind the ball close to their own goal. However, this is different than using this style of play as the point of departure. In this case, it is a tactical variation to deal with these special circumstances.

If you often lose possession of the ball unnecessarily in the 4:3:3-system, then you will be vulnerable against a team who can execute the counter attack with great efficiency. After all, you give the opponent a lot of space behind your defense. Thus you have to be able to count on an excellent defensive line, who are great in the 1:1 duels and are also able to defend space. They must be strong, both mentally and tactically. It is extremely important that the central defender is fast, because the second central defender will move up during the build-up. There will be no one to cover his back.

You must never choose to play 4:3:3 if you do not have fast defenders who excel in the 1:1 duels and who are exceptional in the positional play to dominate large spaces.

An example of where this went wrong is when Morton Olsen and Jan Wouters coached Ajax in the disappointing 1998-1999 season. The defenders lacked the individual qualities to play this system, therefore the surplus of build-up and attacking qualities were null and void. Furthermore, the average qualities of the players in the midfield did not help the cause.

Over the years, Ajax as well as the Dutch national team let go of the pure 3:4:3-system. It remains tough team tactically to carry the play in this system where the central players have to move up and down the field as a tactical unit, especially if you keep giving away a lot of space on your own half. You will then get into trouble at the international level.

It does not matter which organizational form a trainer chooses to use, his creed should always be: to never choose an organizational form that conflicts with the qualities of your team, made under pressure of others or due to the public opinion. In 1988, I experienced the negative consequences of such a decision. After the success at the European Championship, I became the trainer at Bayern Leverkussen in Germany. I gave in to the wish of the club's management to play a Dutch attacking style football, although I did not have the player personnel to execute that system. It turned out to be a fiasco. The players lacked courage and self-confidence, the essential mental pillars to play this attacking concept. Furthermore, they lacked the team tactical maturity to execute this concept successfully. The intention was there, but they lacked the capabilities. The players could not be blamed for this; it was my wrongdoing that got them in this situation! If you want to play an attacking style of football, then you need to start to develop this in the youth football program of your club. You cannot enforce this one day and expect success the next day.

BASIC TASKS WITHIN THE ORGANIZATIONAL FORM

Within every organizational form, the players have to deal with their basic tasks and functions. This is true for the keeper, defenders, midfielders and forwards. It has the highest priority in the team building process that each player performs his basic tasks. The most important basic task for defenders is to defend. The defender does of course have attacking tasks; he may and must at the correct moment get involved in the build-up and the attack. His main basic task remains however, defending, and he may never neglect this task!

In the past, players such as Van Aerle and Van Tiggelen (1988 Dutch national team), could muster the tactical discipline in every game to first concentrate on their basic (defensive) task. A good example of a current top-notch player who seldom neglects his basic task is defender Jaap Stam of Manchester United. Such types of players are invaluable for a team.

Many players have a problem sticking with their basic task, because they want to show off and do too much. For example, the defender who wants to get involved in the build-up and attack at the expense of his defensive task, or midfielders who do not stay close enough to their direct opponent when the other team is in possession of the ball, thus giving too much space away. His basic task demands a different approach. An attacker sometimes shies away from helping in defense or does a poor job at performing this task. Mental aspects do play a role when this occurs.

During an important qualification match against Ireland for the European Championships of 1996, the basic task of the central midfield players Seedorf and Davids was to control the midfield and therefore their direct opponents. Their attacking task was to go deep when possible and support the attackers. Till the moment Holland scored to make it 1-0, there were ample tactical opportunities for them to perform their attacking task. During the second half, Ireland started to take more risks and pushed the midfielders up more often. The Irish did not accommodate anymore to the tactics of the Dutch team. It was during this phase in the match that Seedorf and Davids did not show consideration to their basic task -controlling the midfield.

An essential problem in the training of defenders in the Netherlands is the fact that the priorities are not on learning how to adequately and fiercely eliminate an attacker. This is an art form in itself! The build-up and attacking team functions have the priority over the defensive team function in the Netherlands. Due to this fact, the Dutch defenders lack the qualities to perform their basic task. Of course there are exceptions to the rule.

Various circumstances are possible in which players believe that they have good reasons why they can neglect their basic tasks. I remember the match Feyenoord-RBC from several years ago. It was the first match for coach Arie Haan on the bench of Feyenoord. A lot of Feyenoord players showed off individually, because they wanted to get noticed, therefore teamwork was missing. It became a sloppy match because many players did not play with their head, and this behavior was not corrected from within the team. The team tactical cooperation suffered quite a bit due to the urge of players to individually prove themselves to the coach. You only get noticed by the trainer however, if through performing your basic task perfectly, you are an added value to the team tactical unit! This tendency to neglect the basic tasks is inherent to football players. It is even true that the better the player, the bigger this tendency. He has the desire to play the game his way.

In team building, the creed should be that a player must never do a bad job at his basic task. This should not only be a fundamental rule of the coach, but also of the players. A player can have a bad day, but never due to neglecting his basic task. This will hurt the team, the teams' organization and the efficiency of the performance of the team!

This professional creed does not apply as much to youth teams. Youth players must receive the space for their own interpretation of their task. Coaches of youth teams do need to convince their players that it is necessary to be disciplined about performing their basic task if the team is going to be successful. The examples set by top-notch players in how poorly or how well they perform their basic task has a bigger impact on youth players than a theoretical lecture.

The coach has to assure in the tactic of the match that players can manage to perform their basic task. A good example is the two matches against Russia at the legendary Euro '88 in Germany. We lost the first match because of problems we faced in the center of the field. The Russians linked the fabulous Michailitsjenko to Ruud Gullit. This Russian could cover a lot of ground and he would run away from Gullit as soon as his team regained possession. Due to this fact, Gullit had to chase after Michailitsjenko too much during the first match. He was not able to perform his basic task as attacker and support striker. When we played Russia the second time in the championship match, we made sure that Gullit was able to perform his basic task to support Marco van Basten. Ronald Koeman received the assignment to play closer to Gullit and coach him from this position, telling him when he did and did not have to keep an eye on Michailitsjenko. Koeman had the task of trying to look after this Russian playmaker, allowing Gullit to perform his basic task as the support striker and force the Russians to worry about him as an open attacker.

To have Koeman play closer to Gullit may on paper seem to be a big risk, but it turned out perfectly. This tactical variation in the basic task of Koeman was justified due to his maturity and experience at such a crucial moment. If the Russians would have dominated the game, it would have been a different story. This team tactical flexibility is the result of the extra qualities possessed by the key players.

When a player neglects his basic tasks, as a coach you will have to take immediate action. Again Ruud Gullit is a good example. In 1992, he did not partake in his responsibility as the right wing forward, to stay with the opposing left defender when possession was lost. This was, however, one of the basic tasks of the wing forwards within the team tactical concept, because there was no one to cover for them. Gullit could no longer muster the physical and mental strength to stay with the outside defender when he would move up to participate in the build-up and attack of his team. In such a situation you have two options as a coach: you stick with the original concept and substitute Gullit, or you adapt the concept on the side where Gullit plays and give him someone who will cover for him. In any case, it does not make any sense in this situation to demand the execution of a basic task if the player is not able to physically and mentally perform the task.

Players also have problems with performing their basic task if the opponent deliberately gives them a lot of space. A good example of this happened in the semi-final match against Denmark in Euro '92. Denmark deliberately gave our outside defenders space to do the build-up from the back. In the tactical strategy for this match, I had predicted that this would happen and gave these defenders the assignment to quickly get rid of the ball. They could not muster this during the game. They held on to the ball too long, and dribbled up field instead of playing the ball quickly. When possession was consequently lost, the opponent would have an ocean of space on the outside behind the defense and Denmark took advantage of this with their counterattack and led 2-0.

During halftime I stressed again to the defenders that they should play their basic task and pass the ball more quickly. We performed this better in the second half and were able to tie up the game.

Players who can muster the mental and tactical strength to perform their basic task can never get an 'insufficient' mark for the match and they are considered perfect team players. However, sometimes it means that you do not stand out in the game and receive a low mark from the journalists who cover the match, but never from the coach.

THE BALANCE

A different, very important organizational guideline is that as the coach you are responsible for keeping the team in the right balance concerning defending, building-up and attacking. Sometimes this balance depends on one player. It can be that delicate at the top. Also, the resistances of the match can force a different balance onto the team. One of the toughest team tactical assignments for the coach is to keep the balance in the team. To achieve this he is of course dependent on the player personnel that are available to him.

A familiar example from the past is when Frank Rijkaard took the place of Wim Jonk at Ajax. The controlling qualities of Rijkaard were at that moment more important for the team than the building-up and attacking qualities of Jonk. When Rijkaard was added he created a better balance in the team. The same problem occurred in the Dutch national team when Jan Wouters would play instead of Jonk. Not because Wouters was a better player than Jonk, but because he was better able to perform the basic task of that position in relation to the tasks of the other players at that moment.

A different example is Dani at Ajax when he took the place of the injured Litmanen in the '98-'99 season. Dani was defensively not (yet) mature enough in team tactical aspects to balance out the loss of Litmanen. His strength lay in his role during the build-up and attack. The fans enjoyed the extra qualities of this creative player. When the opponents had the ball, he showed a great effort, but team tactically he was not yet mature enough to take up the correct defensive position. The fans do not notice this, but the coach does. When such a popular player is substituted or does not play at all, then the coach encounters a lot of incomprehension from fans and the media. This could turn into a negative external factor in the psychological team building process. However, the problem is clear to both the coach and the teammates! When playing against a weaker opponent, these shortcomings when the opponent has possession will not always become very clear. However, when playing a top-notch team, the opponent will immediately take advantage of this weak link when they regain possession. The (positive) result of the match is in danger. The coach, as the protector of this result has to correct the situation both to satisfy himself and the team. This is to the regret of the fans and the media who do not comprehend it.

We should not blame other people for this. You need to have a well-trained tactical eye to recognize the balance within a team. A coach watches a match through different eyes than fans or the media. He registers the individual actions and reactions as an interdependent cohesiveness. It is all about details then. Taking the team task in account, a player might have to move a meter to his right or left, forwards or backwards. Fans do not see this and it is not why they came to the stadium. Many trainers lack the courage to take a little bit more risk with such a player. It remains a matter of much deliberation, especially if there are plenty of other players to put in his spot.

An example of such a player, who always disturbed the balance due to the fact that he neglected his basic tasks, was Henk Fraser at Feyenoord-Rotterdam. He was an excellent central defender, but he enjoyed going up in the attack at all moments in the game. He would in particular not stay back anymore after scoring a goal. The opponents counted on him joining into the attack and anticipated this behavior. Compare this to the style of play of Cocu at PSV-Eindhoven, FC Barcelona and the Dutch national team. Cocu always performs his basic task as defensive midfielder or even as a defender, before he picks out the moments when he joins the attack and goes forward. This is why he is regularly able to surprise the opponent and score important goals.

Cocu understands that the ground rule should be that you first take care of your basic task before you try to do more if the situation in the match allows for this to happen. A player needs to be tactically mature before he can recognize these moments in the game (correct timing), individually as well as collectively. Also needed is the correct mental attitude in relation to a player's task and function within the total team. This is a point of view that will get more attention in chapter 4, when we discuss the mental team building process.

At the top-level it is details that count. An example of creating balance in a team is the adaptations made in the organization of the defensive line in the Dutch national team. It appeared that this balance was disrupted when playing with a three-man defensive line, due to the enormous resistance in matches played with the national team, especially at European or World Championship tournaments. Holland was defensively vulnerable in the spaces behind the outside midfielders. It is then a logical step of the coach to try to restore this balance by adding an extra defender to the line. Decisive were the lessons taught by England in 1996, at Wembley stadium. England created a lot of chances by taking optimal advantage of this space on the outsides.

Something that does not negatively influence the team tactical balance while playing matches in the national competition can crush you at the international level. This is also due to the fact that most teams in the national competition use the same team organization.

In 1987, we played a home European Championship qualification match with the Dutch national team against Greece. At that time, I still chose to play with a three-man defensive line, with two defenders as man and space markers and one as a sweeper behind or in front of them depending on the situation. In this concept the spaces on the outside had to be covered by the outside midfielders. On the right side this was the task of Jan Wouters. The Greeks were smart enough to have a right midfielder constantly make diagonal runs into this space. Therefore Jan Wouters had to play more as a right defender than as a right midfielder. This was not his strong point and the balance of the team was therefore more or less disturbed.

At half-time, I tried to make clear to the players that due to the fact that we lost possession of the ball too many times, we could not dominate during the build-up, and that the Greeks were tactically taking advantage of this. We did better in the second half and were able to dominate in the midfield. Wouters was then able to do a good job as the controlling midfielder. Looking at the way the match turned out, if this would have not happened, then I would have had to bring in a defender, maybe even at the expense of an attacker. You need to control the opponent if you want to play an attacking style football!

After the match, there was only one person who agreed with my tactical analyses of the game... Jan Wouters. All the other people were talking about the tactical blunder of the coach who had sent Jan Wouters into the field with an incorrect description of his task.

Of course it is a possibility that you misjudged the strength of the opponent. For example, if an opponent is capable of taking advantage of weak aspects in your style of play, you should then look for tactical variations within your style of play.

During World Cup '94 in the USA, and Euro '96 in England, it appeared that such an intervention was no longer enough to do the trick. One aspect of the style of play needed to be structurally revised: the 3-man defensive line was changed to a 4-man line. Such an intervention of course has consequences for the manpower in the midfield and so on. This can lead to small changes in the defensive, build-up and attacking strategies. At the international level, you can gain a lot from changing details. The coach is the expert in this matter and the players are carrying out the work. The players must have as much insight into their role as possible, taking the flow of the game into account.

Coaches must always find the correct balance between the three team functions: defending, build-up and attacking. This balance, as has already been mentioned, can be disrupted by one player. On the basis of that you could come to the conclusion that there is no room in a top-level team for a star-player who neglects his defensive task or has not mastered this task. I believe that is putting it too strongly. An absolute prerequisite has to be that his teammates accept this behavior. Most of the time this does not happen, especially if there are more star-players in the team. They find it tough to play at the service of one star-player.

Also of influence is the football culture of a certain country or club. Dutch football players are of the opinion that even star-players must do their defensive work. Just think of the problems Romario had at PSV-Eindhoven, or more recently Cruz at Feyenoord-Rotterdam. However, the Romanian team had no problem with playing at the service of Hagi during World Cup '94 in the USA. This was partly due to the fact that he had exceptional qualities to build-up and attack. At Real Madrid, it was not accepted by the other star-players that Hagi played this role. In addition, Real was not able to constantly perform at a high level, and Hagi's performance was dependent on a few moments. In cases like this, teammates are definitely less likely to do the dirty work for someone else. Even world-class players such as Romario and Ronaldo have experienced this. They have to show all they are capable of in every match, otherwise the team will start to be critical of their performance. If a player such as Ronaldo could guarantee that he would score two goals in every match, then the team and the coach would let him do whatever he pleased. In that case, the teammates would happily do the dirty work for him. However, he cannot give them this guarantee, even if he wanted to. This is the reason that next to his basic task, for example scoring goals, other tasks must be developed.

Some critics claim that players such as Ronaldo, Hagi and Dani do not need to perform these extra tasks. They would have to spend too much energy on, for example, these defensive tasks. This is almost an insult to these modern top-athletes, especially if you take the workload of world-class forwards into account in the Italian, Spanish or English competitions, when the opposition has possession. Of course the real star-players do not always feel like defending. Furthermore, this task demands team tactical maturity. In the case that the forward lacks this maturity, then he will unnecessarily waste a lot of energy. He will succeed, however, by playing efficiently in combination with the other players. This efficiency in particular will save energy!

Players also have to perform their task at the moment possession is lost, otherwise you will have to suffer the consequences while playing against a top-notch team.

This is a tough problem for all coaches to deal with. By neglecting to perform his tasks, the star-player endangers the result of the team. However, the star-player is an extra value for the team and he usually has the sympathy of the fans and the media. He is not aware of the fact that a team tactical problem exists. The only solution is to hold many meetings both with the star player and the team. If you do not play the star-player, then a confrontation will occur and that is the last thing a coach would like to see happen. Such a problem did exist between player Seedorf and Real Madrid. This problem happens a lot more often than the general public realizes.

The modern team building process needs players who can put their top qualities to the service of the team and are capable of playing efficient football. This entails that they can oversee in a split-second what is happening on the field and are willing to immediately act in a team efficient manner. If a player is not capable of performing this at the top-level, it will be hard for him to earn a starting position. All you can do as a coach is to bench him and put him in at times when the game allows for him to get playing time. However, it is not always sensible to select players for this cause. These kind of individualists usually have a strong personality and do not accept playing the second fiddle or sitting on the bench, and therefore they are a negative influence on the atmosphere and the team spirit. These motives certainly played a role in the decision of the successful French coach Aimé Jacquet in not selecting a player such as Eric Cantona for the Euro '96 squad.

During Euro '96, I followed the German as a technical committee member of UEFA, and discussed this issue with the then German national team coach Berti Vogts. He told me that he had learned a great deal from the 1994 World Cup in the USA. The average results at this tournament were not caused by a lack of quality within the team, but more by the make-up of the group. This was the lesson for Vogts to not select certain players who were known for the fact that they would not want to play second fiddle for the team. Such measures are certain to arouse reactions from the press that usually side with the players in this matter. Vogts took advantage of this critique by using it to create a close-knit team from the players that he did select for his team in a much quicker fashion. Thus, in fact he was grateful that the press published the responses from these disappointed players.

It would be even better if the leaders within the team also make this their problem and try to positively influence these players. The German problem children in 1996 were Effenberg, Matthäus and Basler.

Sometimes these individualists do not mind playing second fiddle, but they lack the insight in the game to be able to play efficiently when it is asked of them. A good example is Brian Roy when he played at Ajax. You have to, even if the general public has a hard time understanding, let such a player go. For the best interest of the team, you are sometimes forced to make unpopular decisions. The only thing that counts at the top-level is the results of the team. Players demand that you get rid of or tame the disruptive 'elements'. This assignment is part of your job and the players are entitled to this. However, players hardly ever notice their own shortcomings.

The key players of the team are an extension of the coach in the field, and they guard the all important balance. They are capable of adapting to the circumstances on the field that might be a possible threat to the balance. An example of this is the assignment given to Koeman to coach Gullit in the championship game of Euro '88 in Germany. You can ask a player such as Koeman to do this, because he satisfies all the features a key player should possess. It would have been a mistake to give this assignment to a player who is still too busy performing his own basic tasks in such an important match. The key players guard the team tactical qualities both during training and matches.

On the other hand, key players often decide the fate of the coach. Just remember the derogatory remarks made by Ruud Gullit about national team coach Thijs Libregts, who he did not want to lead the team during the World Cup in 1990, in Italy, after he led the team to a successful qualification. Or even more recently, the remarks made by

Ronald and Frank de Boer about the average quality of the training sessions run by Morton Olsen at Ajax. That meant that the Olsen book was closed at Ajax. The board members in charge will almost always side with the (top) players and not with the coach, especially when the results are not very good. A coach must be capable of defending his credibility to be able to carry out his vision and to protect it. You have to remain faithful to your principles, except when that can hurt your status. The result is the only thing that counts and is the deciding factor for your credibility. The struggle for prestige between a coach and a star-player is of no use if the performance level drops. However, sometimes a player will have to be 'sacrificed' to get the team back on track. You will always have to consider what is best for the performance level.

When the result is not the primary purpose, for example with youth teams, then you can hold on to your principles with more distinction.

THE DEFENSIVE TEAM FUNCTION AS THE STARTING POINT FOR THE ORGANIZATIONAL GUIDELINES

Of the three functions within the team building process - defending, building-up and attacking - the defensive team function has the highest priority when creating the correct balance in the team. It is relatively easy to adapt to the opponent. In any case, it is the process that the coach can influence the most. At the top, all players defend, everything is based on not letting the opponents play! In other words: the anti-football process must be taken care of. To not let the opponent get into their rhythm of play through being well organized as a team is the basis for your own build-up and attack, and thus is a prerequisite to receiving the optimal result. To play efficiently and geared to the result takes precedent over playing beautiful football.

We have a hard time dealing with this in the Netherlands. However, this is the reality of football. You can do a good job building-up and attacking, but if your defense is struggling, then your level of performance will be really vulnerable. At times you will be able to have a good game, but the foundation is lacking. If you want to play an attacking style of football, your defense has to be perfectly organized or you will lose the grip on your opponents.

When making the choice to play attacking style football you are always taking risks, because you give the opponent a relatively big space to operate in. You have to make sure that when possession is lost, the whole team plays defense. If one player does not participate in defense, it will then be impossible to play this style. It is a different case if you play counter style football. Defensive mistakes made by Hagi could be compensated because the Romanians kept enough players behind the ball.

When you are playing very offensively with a not so well organized defense, each player has to help defensively when possession is lost to put pressure on the opponent on their half of the field. Not one player can slack off. Furthermore, you are tactically even more vulnerable when losing possession during the build-up on your own half of the field.

The big difference between the Ajax in her golden years and the Ajax in the current season, is that then they were capable of pressuring their opponent on their half of the field. Ajax also tried to play this attacking style football during the 1998-1999 season, but it was not very successful. That team did not possess good man-to-man markers, players who could win the ball at the midfield. The ball was often lost on the midfield during the build-up, and they lacked players who were goal scorers. Then, in fact, the chosen concept of play is not efficient enough. The defensive team function is not working properly.

It was to the credit of Dutch national team coach Guus Hiddink that the accent was shifted more to the defensive team function to be able to get more grip on the opponents. A well organized defensive effort performed by 11 players in a cohesive team tactical unit forms the realistic basis for the building-up and attacking team functions, and therefore for the result.

When I started coaching at 1. FC Köln, I was faced with a team that lost every home game by a big margin. You could then make the choice to install the principles of the Dutch attacking style football. But, I made a different choice. In preparation for my first match with the team against Eintracht Frankfurt, I placed the accent on the defensive organization and practiced during the training sessions how to eliminate their playmaker. In the mind of the Dutch that would be considered a very negative approach to the game, but it worked and we won. Through having a good result in my first game as the coach, the team gained confidence and I gained credibility. This is the best breeding ground to slowly change the accent to the build-up and the attack.

However, the defensive team function was the point of departure. Therefore, we got a grip on our opponents and were able to get to building-up and attacking. This was a much harder and lengthy process though. As regards to the performance, you are bound by the level of talent of the individual players and the balance between the qualities within the team: forwards and midfielders with scoring abilities, creative and controlling midfielders, etc.

I remember well the match for third and fourth place at World Cup '94 in the USA, between Sweden and Bulgaria. The Swedes started the game with a lot of enthusiasm in contrast with the Bulgarians who were already satisfied by even making it this far in the tournament, and had partied a lot. Even a fourth place at this championship was a great result.

It became clear that from the start of the match, the Bulgarian forwards did not feel like performing their defensive tasks when the Swedes were in possession. This angered the Bulgarian sweeper so much that at one point he even stepped off the field. The Swedes easily won the match 4-0, and they could have scored more goals. Whenever the complete team does not participate when the opponents have possession of the ball, you are surely going to lose that match at the top-level; especially when the other team comes out ready to play.

During important international tournaments the necessity to make the defensive team function a priority always surfaces. When examining the performance of the Nigerian team during World Cup '98 in France, it became clear that they were relying too much on their intuition, improvisation, and therefore, on their instinct. They mastered the short-passing game excellently and all the players were technically brilliant. But that is no longer sufficient at the top-level. Each player must understand and perform his tasks within the three team functions of the game, and especially those in the defensive area. If you do not succeed as a coach to make this clear to the players, then it should not come as a surprise when the team is eliminated from the tournament.

You cannot be clear enough as a coach concerning the description and the assignment of the tasks. The team tactical maturity and the very strong team discipline he possesses determine the tactical room of each player. The influence of the coach on the level of performance is the biggest within the described set of organizational guidelines.

There are two more examples that I would like to share with you. During Euro '96 in England, the German team had to deal with players who were injured, especially starting defenders. Their replacements were not real defenders. However, by playing very disciplined they performed very well and did what they had to do. These players were willing to sacrifice themselves for the good of the team. That produced a good result.

At the same tournament, Italy played a preliminary match against the Czech Republic. The Italians started the match as the favored team, but saw a player ejected early on in the match. It took them 20 minutes to get organized defensively. However, the Czechs punished them right away by scoring a counter attack goal. Eventually, this was the cause of the early departure of the Italian team coached by Sacchi. When a team lacks defensive organization, even if only during part of the match, this could be taken advantage of by the opponent. The Italians lacked the team tactical flexibility at that moment to be able to adapt to this changing situation.

STRATEGICAL TEAM TACTICAL GUIDELINES

For me the strategical team tactical guidelines are the general tactical guidelines for defending, building-up and attacking. As a coach you have the choice of two main team strategies; play the counter-attack or carry the play to the opponent, thus choosing a defensive or an attacking style of football. Based on this choice are the defensive, building-up and attacking guidelines.

There are not many coaches who consciously choose to carry-the-play to the opponent at the international level. The Dutch coaches are the exception to that rule.

In the Netherlands, many coaches make the choice for a strategy where they carry the play. In particular, these Dutch coaches will have to realize that this choice means that they have to give more attention to the tactical cohesiveness of the team during training sessions and matches. It also demands high quality coaching. The mental qualities of players, such as coaching each other on the field and having the courage to keep carrying the play, are very important to succeed.

The advantage of this play-making strategy is that you are capable of playing it under all circumstances. You always take the initiative, and you must do that. However, if you fail to carry the play and get under pressure, then the opponent will take advantage of the weak aspects of the style you are playing. The battle to dominate the midfield is the main thing, it does not matter if you are playing at home or away, against an easy or a tough team.

This is not true when choosing to play counter style football. You let the opponent have the initiative. However, if they cannot make the play, then the counter-team has a hard time dealing with the different role they have to play.

The coaches of the Brazilian and French teams chose to play an attacking style of football during World Cup '98, but not to the extreme of the Dutch team. They built more defensive safeguards into their style of play: they provided more cover for each other. The Brazilians and French had better man-to-man markers at their disposal. A detail perhaps, but at the top, details are the decisive factor.

Their colleagues from other countries usually chose to play a counter style of football. The accent shifts to the defensive strategies. In the first place, a good counter attack team needs to have a strong defensive line with players who will remain calm even under high under pressure. These players are good technical defenders, as for example, the Italian defenders. These players do not fear having to play defense in their own 16-meter area. Dutch teams however, do not excel in this, they would rather play defense further away from their own goal and try to regain possession on the opponents' half of the field.

When a counter-attack team regains possession of the ball, certain players will run set patterns so the counter attack will be successful and can be performed at a high tempo. On the other hand, every player can get involved in the counter attack as long as the situation allows for this. It is all about choosing the correct moment to get involved. Due to his age during his last years at Bayern Munich and the German national team, Lothar Matthäus was no longer often involved in the build-up and attack. However, he became more dangerous to his opponents because of this unpredictability factor in his game. Also his predecessor, Sammer was excellent at choosing the correct moments to join in the attack and therefore had a big part in winning the Euro '96 tournament in England.

However, a 'counter team' can also take the initiative, for example, when they are behind in the score or playing a match where they are favored to win. This is then a tactical variation of the general strategies. However, this is not the team's favorite style of play. The situation in the match forces the team to change to this style of play. Usually the coach will substitute a player; for example a forward or attacking midfielder takes the place of a defender. The coach can also choose to change the description of the tasks or the guidelines concerning the defensive, build-up or attacking team function.

A good example of this is the championship match between Germany and the Czech Republic in the Euro '96 tournament in England. It was a match between two teams who both favor counter attack style football. The Czechs put themselves in the underdog position and forced the Germans into becoming the favored team. Thus coach Berti Vogts had to change his tactical plan for the match. This meant that he had to put a bigger emphasis on the functions when his team was in possession of the ball (build-up and the attack). This is not an easy assignment for a counter attack team. When such a team falls behind in the match, they have great difficulty applying more build-up and attacking pressure on their opponent. For example, top-teams from Portugal, the ultimate counter attack teams, will switch over to the traditional English style football with the accent on giving long passes. A central defender with a good heading technique will often play as a second striker.

Dynamo Kiev is an example of a team that has everything you need to be an 'ideal' counter team. This is mostly due to Valeri Lobanovski, whose professional skill I respect a great deal. He selects and develops players with excellent technical abilities, who are capable of very fast transitions from defending to attacking, can perform very quick combinations up front, and are masters in the attacking 1:1 duels and, very importantly, possess the capabilities to finish the chances they create.

GUIDELINES FOR THE PLAY-MAKING STRATEGY

The play-making strategy is not often seen. This style of football is risky to play and needs to have a lot of players with individual qualities. In most football cultures the coaches are scared to use it. And this is not only because of the pressure, both external (media) and internal (board, sponsors and fans). Furthermore, the following slogan usually applies: 'Winning! How is less important.'

England and the Netherlands are the exception to this rule, and to a certain extent also France and some African countries such as Nigeria. Countries in South America? Hardly. Even Brazil reduces risky football. They start almost every match as the favorite to win and they have brilliant players to build-up and attack. However, if they are ahead in the match they start playing more carefully. Even in Brazil, the result rules.

This risky style of play demands individually a lot of football capacity. It entails that you often have to operate in small spaces during the build-up and attack and defend large spaces with few players. This style of play requires a methodical process in the youth program, and also specific types of players; such as the wing forwards and defenders who get involved in the attack in the Netherlands. The most important guidelines are:

DEFENSIVELY

- ▶ When losing possession in the attacking phase, the entire team has to be tactically able to defend. Preferably by keeping the opponents on their own half or by dropping back more if you do not succeed in that. This demands good positional play in tactical coherence with each other.
- ▶ The defensive line needs to push up right away towards the midfielders. In general you defend far away from your own goal.
- ▶ There are 3 or 4 players in the defensive line. The 4th defender will play as a free defender and pushes into the midfield. Defensively this means that you have an extra player to put pressure on the opponent.
- ▶ The 3-man defensive line must be sharp while defending the spaces and they must be fast.
- ▶ The keeper acts as a sweeper when a counter attack team unexpectedly plays a long ball through.
- ▶ The midfield line must have controlling players with tactical insight and discipline who will remain behind the ball during the attack.

- ▸ No player may get passed in his zone. This is especially a point of attention for the defensively vulnerable forwards.
- ▸ Players who can regain the ball are indispensable.

Remark:

At the top of the international football scene I believe the 3-man defensive line is too difficult to operate without an adequate marking of the wings. However, this marking will be at the expense of a well-balanced midfield line. We find this adaptation in the ever-increasing use of the 5:3:2 (or 3:5:2) team structure. There is a good reason why the build-up team function is a vulnarable aspect in this team structure.

BUILDING-UP

- ▸ The team must master the 'ball circulation' component to be able to determine the correct moment to start the attack. However, ball circulation is a means, not a goal in itself! To carry the play on the opponents half of the field places high demands on the build-up. There is not much time and space to work in and you have to deal with high defensive pressure. Fast combinations and excellent positional play are a must. Circulation football!
- ▸ To lose possession close to the middle line when building-up is almost 'suicidal' in this risky style of football.
- ▸ One touch passing is also a must in the building-up team function of this strategy. This demands additional tactical insight from the players as situations quickly have to be surveyed. Each player has to anticipate even more.
- ▸ To carry the play means that one time you choose to play in a high tempo and the next time you use delaying tactics to slow the play down.
- ▸ A play-making-team must take full advantage of the space and must have defenders who can quickly change the point of attack, wing forwards who remain on the outside, etc.
- ▸ The transition from defense to build-up must be executed very quickly.
- ▸ The team tactical manpower in the center of the field (central defenders, midfielders and striker) is of great importance. During the build-up, the tactical coherence between the central defenders who must be thinking of playing the ball forward, the attacking midfielders and the central striker is very precise work. When possession is lost, it starts in the opposite direction.
- ▸ Good ball circulation puts high demands on the quality of the positional play, the mastering of the tempo and the speed of action.

ATTACKING

▶ There are three possible attacking lines in the build-up. They have to be utilized as varied as possible. This depends mostly on the organizational form, the allocation of tasks and functions, and the quality of the players.

▶ Two of these attacking lines run over and down the flanks, on the right and left side. They can, but do not have to be identical. This usually depends on the quality of the players involved and the chosen organizational form.

▶ One of these attacking lines runs down the center of the field.

These attacking lines will be talked about in more detail in the continuation of this chapter when dealing with 'attacking strategies'.

GUIDELINES FOR THE COUNTER ATTACK STRATEGY

The accent in the counter attack style of play lays on the defensive team function, with the emphasis being on the defender's own half of the field and letting the opponents keep the initiative of the game. This is to take advantage of the space that opens up behind their defense for the build-up and the attack. The most important guidelines are:

DEFENSIVELY

▶ When the team has the time to organize, they will fall back on their own half of the field.

▶ When attacking, more players are and will remain behind the ball in comparison to in front of the ball.

▶ There is limited space between the goal and the defensive line.

▶ On your own half, the marking remains aggressive.

▶ The spaces between the defensive, midfield and forward lines are as limited as possible. This is a matter of creating a compact defensive block.

▶ The midfield line acts as the first line of defense. They must keep the opponents in front of their zone. This midfield line plays close to the defensive line and thus defends on their own half of the field.

▶ To be able to defend under the pressure of the opponents requires good man-to-man markers and levelheaded defenders.

▶ To be able to defend under the pressure of the opponents, it is also required that the tactical coherence between the defenders is optimal. In that manner, you can close down the operational attacking space of the opponents.

BUILDING-UP

▶ The emphasis within the build-up of the counter attack strategy lies in taking advantage of the space behind the defense of the opponents. This demands, besides controlling the set patterns, the tactical insight to profit from the game situations. You need to have a few very fast players in your team when playing the counter attack style.

▶ They prefer to win the ball during the build-up of the opponents.

▶ When forced to build-up from the back, a super fast transition is required, including good positional play in a fast manner and in a forward direction.

ATTACKING

▶ Mostly, the fast target player who is good with the ball will be the basis. With the big spaces around him he remains an important target to play the ball to. He takes the pressure off his team by being able to quickly receive a long pass.

▶ A characteristic is the overlapping midfielders and deep sprinting attackers who have a good sense for the tactical spaces and timing.

▶ Many actions are performed at full speed, which is an added difficulty. The trick is to still get the optimal result out of the counter attack. Usually the finishing on goal is done too hastily.

Remarks:

▶ Counter attack football places high demands on the team tactical and mental qualities of players.

▶ Counter attack football is easier to train. For example, you are able to start earlier in building set patterns in comparison to the play making strategy.

▶ When being behind in the game, a counter attack team has trouble taking the initiative. Against a weaker team, the coach will have to fall back on a more attacking variation of his counter attack style of play. Most of the time this is not very well mastered. They lack the set patterns in their style of play and the specific players to perform this. On the other hand, a play-making team must also be able to fall back on the tactical counter attack variation. However, this is mastered much more easily.

To summarize:

Every coach has to decide for himself which style of play he will utilize: the play- making style or the counter attack style. Then he has to determine in which organizational form he wants to perform it: 4:3:3, 4:4:2 or 5:3:2. The 4:3:3 system is not as suitable to counter attack football.

Then he describes the tasks of the players during the defensive, build-up and attacking team functions. Next, he indicates the most important strategies within the three team functions through a set of guidelines. In every match, a tactical variation of the style of play will usually be utilized, depending on the expected opposition and the desired result.

Counter attack football has shown to be the most efficient when short-term success is desired. Thus, let the opponent carry the play and take advantage of mistakes made by the opponent to utilize the counter attack strategies. Egil Olsen, the former national team coach of Norway, has been able to prove statistically the success of this approach. Thus Norway plays this distinct style of counter attack football with all their national teams. This is also a true statement for the Norwegian club football.

MY PERSONAL CHOICE

As a coach I have personally always made the choice to use the play-making strategy. Around the famous World Cup '74 in Germany, I wanted to enforce the strength of our attacking by utilizing a new defensive strategy: namely to lock the opponents on their own half of the field! Disturb their build-up in an early phase to regain possession of the ball as quickly as possible. By making that choice, I put us under a big time restraint. A preparation period of 5 weeks to install such a daring strategy is very short. I mostly had to deal with players from Ajax-Amsterdam and Feyenoord-Rotterdam, and one individual (Rob Rensenbrink) from a different club.

At the first team meeting I explained every detail of this tactical variation to all the players. I also told them about the risks involved. Everyone was aware of the fact that it would be difficult to perform this variation perfectly with such a short time to prepare. If some of the players had doubted this variation at the start of the preparation period, then I would have abandoned it. To be able to play this defensive variation, all players have to participate. I also made them aware of the fact that this variation would be tough to carry out for the Feyenoord players. These players from Rotterdam were used to the slow build-up orchestrated by Willem van Hanegem. To be able to play the faster circulation style football in the chosen concept, the tempo would have to be raised quite a bit.

I told the players during the first team meeting: "This choice is the most difficult one, but for the real football lover also the most beautiful one. We can do it if everyone stands behind it 100 percent. However if some of you doubt that we are capable of doing it, then we will not adopt this. I can give you the guidelines but you will have to perform it on the field." The group showed an immediate eagerness to take on this challenge. If you are able to link a team to a concept, then that will function as a team motivator and a team building factor.

During the preparation phase, we consciously played many games against amateur teams. They are automatically forced into playing more defensively on their own half of the field with a lot of players behind the ball. You end up in the same situations that you will face at the World Championships, with of course less resistance. We repeated all the basic principles of this concept over and over again. After every match, the players and I would discuss what went right and wrong.

Next you try out the variation in friendly matches against other national teams. This did not turn out too well in the beginning. For example, against Austria the performance was very disappointing. We were surprised by the counter attacks of the opponent. Immediately the criticism from external forces increased. However, the group kept their faith in it. During the second friendly match against Argentina, played at the Olympic stadium in Amsterdam, it suddenly went well. We won 4-1. If we had not been successful, then I would have made changes to the concept. We would not have pressured the opponent on their half of the field.

Also, during the first match at World Cup '74 in Hannover against Uruguay, the chosen strategy worked out. This remained so until the championship match. The two teams in the final, Germany and the Netherlands were well matched against each other, although both teams utilized a different tactic in this match. When that happens, the finishing touch of an individual world-class player will be the deciding factor. Unfortunately for the Netherlands, the finishing touch came from the foot of Gerd Müller and not Johan Cruijff.

At FC Barcelona, I also chose to use the play-making strategy. When you start working at such a famous club, then you know that the result is the only thing that is important. Which style of play you use is less important. However, everyone expected Barcelona to play like Ajax did. They did not realize that such a team building process takes years to develop.

However, because Barcelona had played with typical outside forwards under the guidance of the English coach Vick Buckingham, the choice for the 4:3:3 system was not too difficult to make. It was harder to find the right player for the right position. After a process of many years at Ajax to find the correct balance, it was more difficult than expected to achieve this at Barcelona. We succeeded defensively, however the individual qualities were disappointing concerning the build-up and the attack. Nevertheless, the extended Barcelona-family and the media would always speak of the players at Barcelona as the best group of players in the world...

To sharply formulate the tasks and functions within the thee team functions and the battle array (4:3:3) constitutes the first step. It took more time to adapt the team tactical guidelines to the reality of everyday life, especially when taking the specific Spanish circumstances into account. Every match in the national competition is a championship match and ... a battle!

At the start it was difficult for several players to play disciplined and stick to their basic tasks first. We lost a lot of points in that period. It does not fit in with the character of many Spanish players. They always want to show something extra, even if it hurts the team interest. Spanish players have a tough time dealing with criticism. Because of the enormous attention for the Spanish top clubs in the daily newspapers, the chance of getting regularly criticized is pretty good. The players had the tendency to create little 'kingdoms' on the field so they would be sufficiently noticed in a positive way. It is great for the coach and the team if players are conscious of their task, however it does not yield many points in the individual list of rankings made up by the media. Having this knowledge as a coach, it is obvious that an important point of attention during the first few months working at a new top-club is that players need to learn to play conscious of their task in the team's best interest.

However, the priority was on the defensive tactical team function. Pretty quickly, I started to develop an important part of the build-up tactical team function: when possession is lost, move up quickly and put immediate pressure on the player with the ball. There are advantages for both defensive and building-up aspects. Defensively this means that you quickly get away from your own goal and penalty area and for the build-up it means that you create a counter attack situation when the ball is regained.

There are, as always, disadvantages that belong to these advantages. When you push up quickly you become defensively vulnerable when the opponent is given the time to play an intelligent long ball to a deep sprinting player. The essential guidelines for this team tactical aspect are:

▸ Everybody has to help in putting pressure on the ball.
▸ When this is not successful, the defensive line has to reorganize itself.
▸ The signal to react must be given by the clear situation in the game, with the vocal support of the keeper, who also 'moves up', and the central defender.

It takes months of practice to be able to perform this well. You have to keep rehearsing this. For example, during a scrimmage in training, the coach plays a high ball to the defenders. When they head the ball away they have to put immediate pressure on the player with the ball. Or, the coach stands behind the defensive line and throws the ball over them to the opponent. The advantage of such training is that the trainer can decide where and who should be pressured. When the Barcelona team mastered this part of the match in great detail, it became an added value for our style of play. The fans really enjoyed this kind of pressure we put on our opponents.

At the height of the AC Milan period, Baresi was a great initiator to have everyone push up in such situations and put an enormous pressure on the player in possession of the ball.

Remarks:

▸ While going over this component, I have taken special notice of the team building process at FC Barcelona to make the style of working and the objectives clear once more. It is not a trick I use, but a realistic part of the match with more advantages than disadvantages. As long as it is perfected in great detail. This can only be realized by trial and error.

▸ I used to be and still am a proponent of a style of play where the emphasis is put on the attacking team function (supported by specific strategies that will be gone over at a later stage in the book). In both 1974 and 1988, this style of play brought us the ultimate success.

STRATEGICAL GUIDELINES PER TEAM FUNCTION

After the coach has made the choice for a counter-attack or play-making style of play, the general tactical guidelines or strategies need to be addressed concerning the three different team functions.

DEFENSIVE STRATEGIES AS THE BASIS FOR
YOUR TEAM TACTICAL GUIDELINES

Putting pressure on the build-up of the opponent:
▸ With a play making style of play: preferably on the half of the opponent (sometimes the opponent forces you to make a tactical adaptation).
▸ With a counter attack style of play: preferably on your own half of the field (also here the opponent may force you to make a tactical adaptation).

- In the past, coaches sometimes chose a third option: to build a wall of defenders about 35 meters from their own goal. You seldom see this today. An exception could be a team that is pushed with their backs against a wall during the final 15 min. of the game, trying to hold on to a lead. It is all about a team tactical variation, based on the kind of match and the course of the match at that moment. In preparation for the match, this aspect has usually been practiced extensively.

- The most difficult aspect is to put pressure on the opponent early on as a defensive block in the opponent's half of the field. This choice is still, however, made quite a lot in the Netherlands. With this form of pressure football, also known as 'hunting the opponent', the first player who puts pressure on the opponent in possession hardly ever wins the ball. The second player is usually also too late, due to the fact that the opponent usually plays a square ball or plays it backwards. The third player has the best chance of being able to challenge for the ball. Also, you can often observe that the first and second player, after pressuring the ball, do not sufficiently take part in winning back the ball. It is essential that they take up a different position depending on the situation created by the third player. When the ball is played back to the goalkeeper, a different team tactical situation develops. Also in that situation, players keep 'hunting' the ball. To learn to put pressure on the opponent early on does not only demand mental and physical willingness of players, but especially asks for insight into the situation in close team tactical coherence. This shows how difficult the execution of this choice is. Most teams therefore choose to place the defensive block around the middle line. From that position forward they put pressure on the opponent. A prerequisite to being able to pressure the opponents as a team unit is that the three lines play close together to limit the operating space of the opponent in between the lines.

ORGANIZATIONAL FORM

By drawing up defensive strategies for the three lines, the organizational form and style of play do of course have an impact on this process. Considering the team structure, several organizational forms are possible for the defensive line. For example, the English-Swedish model: four defenders on a flat line, without specific man-markers. Each defender picks up the opponent in his area.

In the Italian model, one of the defenders plays as the sweeper, such as Baresi did at AC Milan. An outside defender or the sweeper will in alternation pick up the second forward. The Italians will place three defenders in the center when they are under pressure from the attackers. One of the outside backs will help out in the center depending on how the attack develops. The defending tasks on the wings will have to be performed by midfielders. This so called 'tilting' requires a lot of running from the midfielders, good timing, and a fast transition when the ball has been won.

Another possibility is to have a 4-man defensive line where one of the central defenders plays behind or in front of the other 3 defenders, depending on the situation.

The toughest organization for a defensive line is when there are only three defenders. The fourth man will play as a free defender in the midfield. Due to the width and depth of the field, these three defenders must possess the qualities of a man-marker, be able to cover large spaces, and be fast. It demands a lot of tactical insight and courage to play without having cover at your back.

Franz Bechenbauer, as mentioned earlier, orchestrated the German organizational form for the defensive line: two wing players are added to the three man defensive line. Two pure man-markers and a sweeper play in the center. On the outsides are players who have to take care of the whole wing. This option has some advantages in the defensive aspect, but you will come across difficulties during the build-up. As mentioned earlier, there are too many players positioned in the width of the field, which means you now are lacking depth.

The final decision of which organizational form to use is up to the coach. It is one thing to decide which defensive organizational form to use, including the individual tasks and functions. The actual execution of it, in the ever-changing game situations, where players have to make split-second decisions concerning the build-up and attacking activities of the opponent, is a different story. In particular in that situation, it is important that there is good cooperation between the players in the defensive line. Furthermore, there is always a link between the defensive line and the defensive contributions of the midfield and forward lines. The better the development of the defensive positional play, in whatever organization, the better the results. This result is inseparably linked to the specific individual qualities of the defender.

POSITIONAL PLAY

An important team tactical detail is the positional play of the defensive block, not only limited to the defensive line. The better the midfielders and forwards assist in defending, the better the defensive result of the defensive line will be. The defensive positional play is the easiest to train. During the training sessions, a much tougher assignment is the creation of match realistic pressure from the opponent. The coach can receive a lot of support if he has a key player in the defensive line that can be an extension of the coach in the field, not only during matches, but also in the team tactical training sessions.

In the years when AC Milan was a dominant team, Baresi was an ideal example of such a key player. At Milan the team tactical facet of 'tilting' was mastered perfectly.

The individual qualities determine without a doubt the limits of the performance level, defensively, as well as the build-up and the attack. This does not mean that you cannot make considerable progress by adequately repeating team tactical aspects in training.

MARKING

Another important detail is the marking of a forward when he drops back into the midfield. How far do you go with him? As a defender you have to possess the insight to be able to judge if a forward is trying to lure you away to create space for another player, or is he an important play-maker in the build-up?

The guideline is usually: stay with him, but not too far. 'Not too far' rests mostly on the tactical insight of the defender. The set of directions from the coach is the guideline for this player. In training sessions, the coherence with the teammates considering this aspect will be further developed. That is how the team tactical team building process functions, whether this concerns a detail or the big picture.

There are coaches who still tell their defenders to stay with their direct opponent wherever he goes. This choice does not fit in anymore with the developments in modern day football. The further away from your own goal you defend, the more it comes down to covering the spaces in conjunction with your teammates. The closer to your own goal you are defending, the tighter and sharper you have to man-mark. The only thing that counts is to prevent them from creating a chance to score. It happens too often that defenders are surprised by an action of an opponent in their own penalty box. However, it is not that easy, because the attacker has the advantage of being able to choose the moment when he makes the action. Amongst other qualities, a specific quality of defenders is that they are excellent in staying concentrated. Being a fraction of a second too late could mean a chance to score has been created.

Which guidelines have I presented so far to aid in the defense?
▸ A type of support must always be present, even if it is just the goalkeeper!
▸ The pinching in (covering to the inside of the field) and tilting

(by the defense and the midfield) is a precise job in a well oiled team tactical machine;

▶ To cover an opponent by staying with him should not lead to the disorganization of the defensive block;

▶ In the final phase of the attack, you will have to stay with your man. There is no time to survey the situation to give your man off to another teammate;

▶ On the other hand: the further away from your penalty box, the better it is for the positioning of the players on the field, when you cover your own zone. All the players are linked together by invisible pieces of string. The better the positional play, the harder it will be for the opponent to disrupt your organization;

▶ To stay with your mark up the field has clear team tactical limits;

▶ A conductor is of great value in a defensive orchestra;

▶ It is an advantage to push up as a team and gain territory when a ball is cleared;

▶ Good defensive assistance from midfielders and forwards ensures that the defensive line does not have to improvise as much;

▶ Defensive team tactically the lines must play close together.

Remark:

To stay with a mark and pressuring the opponent are team tactical aspects that apply to all teams. The vision of the coach determines the way it is executed. This phenomenon has a big impact on the quality of how football is played. The result is that, both individually and team tactically, the quality demands placed on players and the team are higher than ever.

Two aspects of defending I would like to bring to your attention are: offside and the 'covering defense':

OFFSIDE TRAP AS A TEAM TACTICAL ASPECT

This should not be confused with pushing up when a ball is cleared. However, that could also result in putting the opponents in the offside position. Actually what we mean here is when the defensive line stays flat next to each other as long as possible and pushes up at the exact moment in the final attacking phase of the opponents, when it is possible to lure the forwards into being offside. This does not relate to the cleared ball by the defense, but to the attacking phase of the opponents. It is of course, a possibility that offside can occur after the opponent regains possession after the defense has cleared a ball and pushes up quickly.

The crowning of 'Total Soccer' (1974)

Royal attention for royal soccer (1974)

This team tactical aspect is a strong defensive weapon. It is used frequently by teams who are not favored to win. It is a good tactic to use against a 'long passing team' with forwards who make deep runs. In scrimmages during practice, it is a favorite tactic of the defense, because then they do not have to run as much. I did not like it much myself. The positional play needs to be perfectly organized, but many defenders think that putting up their hand is enough. In that situation, they act without acknowledging the influence of the actions of their teammates. Again, it is a strong defensive weapon, but it demands a lot of training concerning the positional play and sticking with the agreed on plan when to pull the trap. You also need a lot of coaching, and a leader on the field while adapting to the qualities of the opponent.

For me there is a big difference between playing the offside trap as a defensive block or as an individual. Thus, given a situation with few attackers and defenders in a big space where you can easily survey the situation, I am definitely all for using this weapon.

It is about making a clear plan of tactical instructions. The attacking situation must be the identifying 'signal' for everyone to pull the trap. This demands an enormous amount of practice in scrimmages, friendly matches, and in specific team tactical drills and watching those again on video.

With the national team, I did not allow the defensive line to play the offside trap. With such a national team, you have to deal with a defensive line that is made up of players from different clubs. The time to prepare is too short to adequately train the offside trap. I did, however, allow my defenders to pull the individual offside trap if the situation allowed for it.

COVERING DEFENSE

It is important that there is an arrangement made by the coach concerning what I call the 'covering defense': which players should always remain behind the ball when you are building-up or attacking? When, at the top-level, too few players remain behind the ball, you will be punished without mercy. You are asking to get scored on through a quick counter attack.

In my arrangement, the organization of the 'covering defense' would be based on a 4-block and a 6-block. The six players would be allowed to be involved in the build-up, but the 4 players need to stay disciplined and remain behind the ball at all times. These four players do not necessarily have to be the back four. The bigger the movements between the three lines, the more positional changes there will be. 'Total football' is based on this principle.

There are a lot of misunderstandings about this team tactical aspect. The fact that a number of players remain behind the ball is being confused with the idea that two or more players cover only one attacker while the team is building-up.

The 'covering defenders' cover more than just the one or two deep forwards; they also cover the operational spaces. Thus, spaces where a cleared ball can end up or space that an opposing defender can utilize if he quickly counter attacks. These spaces will have to be covered. The big mistake that is made with this is that the 'covering defenders' do not participate and pay attention to what happens in the build-up and the attack in front of them. Also, they need to be constantly moving and taking up positions up the field in coherence with their teammates in the build-up and the attack. Too many times in this phase, these 'covering defenders' are acting too much as spectators.

When you want to execute it perfectly, a 'covering defender' should tactically be able to take part in the build-up and the attack. He then will play in front of the ball and his position will be taken over by a teammate. I have to admit that this is a facet that is not very well developed with most teams. However, this is an indispensable part of the so-called 'Total football': high-grade positional play, so that 10 players are constantly involved in the build-up and the attack, without neglecting the 'covering defense'. This also means that when possession is lost, 10 players (and the goalkeeper) must quickly and team efficiently transition. This is for all players the most beautiful football there is. Exceptionally difficult, it demands endless hours of training with team discipline as a definite requirement. Obviously here it is also true: the better the players, the more you are able to achieve.

For me, the guideline concerning the 'covering defense' was: 4 players. When we were forced to take more risks, due to the score or the course of the match, then 3 players in the 'covering defense' was the minimum. Naturally the striker is covered very tightly by one or even two players. One of them anticipates the space in front and keeps a close eye on the line between the ball and the striker. In any case, a team must be a constantly positional searching unit. This is an art in itself that takes a lot of work, but is well worth the effort!

Every coach can organize the 'covering defense' in his own way. It is however important that there are guidelines that are rehearsed in training. For example, scrimmages in which the realistic game situations are being simulated. These sessions cannot be too long; they demand an optimal concentration and motivation. You cannot ask this from the players for too long a period of time, because the challenge of the actual game is lacking. It does not matter how well you have simulated the game situation!

BUILD-UP STRATEGIES

To be able to raise the performance level in modern day football, it is absolutely necessary to have fast transitions from defending to building-up/attacking and the other way around. Most top-teams choose to have a very fast transition from defending to building-up/attacking.

The organization in the build-up needs to create situations to be able to play the ball deep as quickly as possible. I would like to stress that as quickly as possible also means as advantageous and effectively as possible. Thus, it does not mean, as described in the English style, as simple and opportune as possible via a long ball. In my view, the deep ball may not be played blindly or compulsively. It should not be based on coincidence. By playing the ball in a well thought out manner, the chance to succeed will be greater. Sometimes this means playing a direct long ball. Other times you choose to make use of more 'stations' to get to the attacking pass. With this pass the attacking phase starts.

Most European and South American countries strive for achieving an attacking action through a deliberate build-up. However, in Great Britain and Norway, the long pass without a true build-up is the dominant style of play. You can, however, observe in some British top-teams such as Arsenal, Chelsea, Glasgow Rangers and Manchester United, a tendency for a more deliberate build-up. Counter attack teams also make frequent use of the long ball, but this choice is alternated with a calm build-up from the back if the counter attack is not on.

Coaches and players will have to realize that 'midfield play' is a means to be able to play the ball deep, and not an aim in itself! This is a golden rule, but difficult to interpret under the ever changing circumstances!

In preparation for Euro '88, the emphasis was often placed on the long ball during training sessions of the Dutch team, to be able to sharpen this attacking weapon. It was practiced in scrimmages: 'try to play the long ball, however, not to the expense of the accuracy. Choose the correct moment to pass.' We practiced this in scrimmages that lasted 20 minutes. I would tell the players how long the matches were and that I demanded of them that they had to give all they had. These 9v9 matches were played on the edge of life and death. They were fantastic to watch. The players were not able to keep it up longer than the 20 minutes. Thus, it needs to be repeated over and over again to get the players to fully understand the power of this tactical weapon. When the tournament began, I stopped running these sessions. The minds of the players were too much on the matches and so you have to train less specifically. They are not able to gather the motivation and concentration to work on this team tactical aim.

CIRCULATION FOOTBALL

Circulation football is the name for a specific build-up style. Not many top-teams master this well. This strategy is distinguished by the ability to circulate the ball from player to player until the correct moment arises for the attacking phase and thus, the ball can be played deep. That moment can arise very quickly, but it can also take many passes over many stations. This strategy only then makes sense, and is only efficient when it starts a good attacking phase.

As has been said before, only a few teams master this style. It places a high demand on the build-up qualities of the team, together with high-quality positional play. This is a tough assignment, especially if the opponents pressure you constantly.

Circulation football is linked to two guidelines:

▶ It is a means to be able to play the ball deep and not an aim in itself.

▶ It has to be linked to a healthy dose of opportunistic football via for example, the lucky pass and the cross.

The coach who 'forgets' these guidelines when playing circulation football chooses to play boring football, without many surprises and thus is easy to defend.

During World Cup '98 in France, in the global confrontation between the best teams, only a few teams mastered the circulation football style as it should be played in my opinion. France, Brazil, the Netherlands, Argentina and - surprisingly - also England and Marokko. In the golden years of Ajax, they were able to perform this style to perfection, just as FC Barcelona. Mainly, the groundwork for this must be laid in the youth football years. This is why coach Louis van Gaal fell back on Dutch players while at Barcelona. In comparison to Spanish players, they were trained in the principles of this style while they were young players. A structural approach in the youth education system of Barcelona could lead to some success, but a top-team such as Barcelona will always be dependent upon the global market for its players.

KICK AND RUN

The counterpart of circulation football is the refined kick and rush football as seen mostly in England, Scotland and Norway. However, top-teams from these countries are putting more elements of circulation football in their game. As coaches though, we can not forget that the spectators in England enjoy watching these kick and run games. There is always something happening around the penalty box.

OPPORTUNISM

Opportunism is the third strategy for the build-up. There needs to remain space in football for a surprising action in the build-up and the attack. This is possible through opportune plays. You need to have the courage in the attacking third of the field to sometimes 'blindly' cross the ball and not choose to play a square pass or a back wards pass. We can all still remember the gorgeous goal scored by Marco van Basten against the Russians in the championship match of Euro '88. However, the cross given by Arnold Mühren, to assist in this goal, was very opportune! I miss this opportunism often in Dutch teams. It sometimes seems like they only want to score a goal out of very elaborate combination play. Perhaps they will succeed at times, but most of the time it does not work.

Another example is the Colombian national team. They were said to be a dangerous threat before World Cup '94 by several experts, amongst others Johan Cruijff. However, the Colombians exaggerated the short combinations to the extent that the opponents had ample time to organize their defense. In the style they played, there was no opportunism, thus it lacked the surprise element.

I believe that when you have a chance to cross the ball into the box, that you should take full advantage of that situation and play the cross. I have had discussions about this with outside forwards during my period at Ajax. The player wondered what good it would do if he crossed the ball when there were no teammates in front of the goal. I made it clear to him that this was not his problem. When nobody is positioned in front of the goal after a good cross is given, I can confront the other forwards with this. When the cross is not given at all, then the next time they will not make the run on time.

In the period between 1980-1983, I chose to play a 4:4:2 with a deliberate build-up as the basic concept when coaching at 1. FC Köln. However, if there was a disappointing score in the game, especially at home games, with only 20 minutes to play, then we would switch to a more opportune approach. Namely, to a more kick and run strategy. When such a situation occurred, the team had to get the ball into and around the penalty box as soon as possible, preferably with crosses from the wings. My sweeper would act as an extra forward in the center; he was strong in the air. The opponents were constantly put under pressure in and around the opponents' box. There were only three defenders left over who were not allowed to take part in the build-up or the attack.

The advantage of this 'English style' football was that the crowd would get behind the team, because we were constantly putting attacking pressure on the opponents. This style of play also prevented the ball from being lost in an early stage in the midfield. This does happen a lot in the final minutes of a game, if you are losing and sticking to a deliberate build-up.

Such an opportune style of play may seem simple to perform, but it is not. You will have to practice it many times in a game realistic atmosphere in training. Practice it so all the players will comply with the guidelines. In addition, it is hard for a coach in a stadium to give the signal to the team to switch over to the more opportune strategy. The signal I used most of the time was to substitute a player.

This opportune approach produced some success for 1. FC Köln in important matches.

DETAILS

I will go over the build-up strategies in more detail. I will start with the role of the defensive line. For example, you could choose the Brazilian option: one of the two outside defenders always gets involved in the build-up. A midfielder and the central defenders will compensate for this as has been earlier described. The central defenders will only perform their defensive tasks. You could observe this by watching Brazilian defender Santos when he played at Ajax. They expected him to have mastered the covering of space and that he would also take part in the build-up. However he did not master this. This was understandable when looking at his past as a man-marker in Brazil. This relegated him to the Ajax bench, while he was a starter for the Brazilian national team.

The opposite occurs too. We sometimes see 'older' written-off Italian players blossom when they transfer to English teams, such as Zola at Chelsea. Chelsea is an example of an English club that chooses to play a more deliberate build-up. To be able to do this, you need a specific type of player, Zola is a master of this style of build-up. He receives a bit more space in the English competition than he did in Italy. He regained his motivation and at once became an invaluable player for Chelsea. At that time, the English top-strikers were not very successful in the Italian competition. The razor-sharp marking and a different style of play were the causes of their failure. Modern day football possesses plenty of these examples. Brilliant players in one style of play fail to shine in the next one.

It is typically Dutch to choose to create a situation where there is a numerical advantage in the midfield by letting the sweeper push up. This player has a lot of space and will be a key player in the build-up. Ronald Koeman and Danny Blind are examples of players who mastered this perfectly. They recognized the correct moment to push-up, after which Ronald Koeman could profit from the long pass he was able to give, especially to the wing players. To Danny Blind this was a bit more difficult, but he was of great value to Ajax in the build-up. The same was true for Wim Jonk. Guardiola plays this role at Barcelona. We can observe something similar in a different system (3:5:2). German top player Sammer played a key role in the European success of Borussia Dortmund and the German national team at Euro '96, while performing this task. Also, German Lothar Matthäus, who holds the German record for most international matches played, used to be excellent at performing this role. In the Dutch style, only one central defender stays back and in the German style two will remain back.

In case the opponent takes counter measures by marking this playmaker, you will have to locate an open midfielder who can play the long ball. Due to the close marking in the midfield, it would be better if this is a player who moved up from the defensive line. Most (international) opponents do not have an extra player in the midfield to cover such a player. They usually do not dare to push a player from their own defensive line up into the midfield.

FORMATION

The most classical formation of the midfield is the 'diamond' shape.
▸ In the 4:4:2 organization there will be a central midfielder who has a defensive task, a controlling left and right midfielder, and a more attacking midfielder who plays behind the two forwards. In fact, this formation is most clear when talking about the allocation of tasks and functions. The Brazilians used this formation in 1998. However, this formation is used less nowadays than before. It has become defensively more vulnerable. The solution most often used is one deep forward and one close behind him who operates more from the midfield. This is instead of two deep forwards and an attacking midfielder.
▸ Also, in the most attacking style of play, 3:4:3, there is a diamond shaped midfield formed by the free player in the midfield, a controlling midfielder on the left and right side, and an attacking midfielder close behind the central forward. In this organization there are also two outside forwards. Most essential in this option are the tactical distances between the players in the central part of the field (free player, attacking midfielder, central forward) during defending, building-up and attacking.
▸ A second option (in the 4:4:2 -concept) can be observed in British and Italian teams: they have two outside and two central midfielders. Defensively this is an excellent choice, because these four players can cover the complete width and length of the field. The outside midfielders do have to cover a large area in the build-up and the attack. One of the central midfielders plays a more defensive role and is the playmaker, while the

other one plays more as an attacking midfielder who supports the two forwards. In the more defensively focussed Italy, it is tough to support the forwards because they stay too far up front. Sometimes the outside midfielders are not being involved enough in the build-up. As said before: 'every team organization has its advantages and disadvantages in the build-up'. There is still a lot of work to do in this area.

▶ The third option deals with the midfield-formation of the 3:5:2 concept. In fact 5 or 6 players are involved in the build-up. A certainty is the two couples on the left and right side of the field. One of them is more defensively oriented and covers the whole flank. The other plays more centrally and has a more attacking role. In between these 4 midfielders plays a more defensively oriented 'anchor man'. With so many midfielders it is difficult to find the right individual man for the right spot.

Many variations are possible in these three options depending on the views of the coach and the available pool of players.

PREREQUISITES

Whatever strategy you choose as a coach, your midfield will always have to satisfy five important prerequisites:

▶ First of all the midfield, as the secondary defensive line, cannot be too vulnerable. The midfielders have to perform their tasks in a disciplined manner.

▶ Secondly, while attacking, the operational spaces on the outside will have to be managed by the midfielders in good cooperation with the outside defenders, possibly the outside attackers and the central forwards.

▶ Furthermore, it is important that the correct player in the midfield play the long ball at the correct moment.

▶ Another midfielder has to decide at which moment it is possible to sprint up the field without the ball. Such a player is very hard to cover, due to the fact that he is moving into space, instead of already standing there.

▶ The covering defenders must stay alert where they position themselves in the build-up and attacking phases, and depending on the developing situation, can regain a ball that is cleared or participate in the build-up or attack at any given moment.

ATTACKING STRATEGIES

When discussing attacking strategies, I have to give notice that the distinction between the build-up and attacking strategies can not always be determined. In certain situations it is difficult to determine if it is the end of the build-up or the beginning of the attack, they overlap. As mentioned before, in the strategies that have to be developed within the attack, three attacking lines are most important: the left wing, the right wing and the line through the center.

ATTACKS OVER THE FLANKS

- There is a clear distinction between playing with or without permanent outside attackers. The outside attacker is expected to be able to get past his opponent with speed and give a good cross to incoming teammates: at the near post or in other spaces inside or outside the penalty box. These high-speed actions place high demands on the individual technique, tactics, and physical qualities of these outside attackers.

- Only a few players master the technique to cross a ball with 'feeling'. The cross is often not delivered correctly because the outside attacker loses the oversight of the situation, and/or lacks the technical qualities. One of the most difficult ingredients of the attacking game is to deliver a good cross. It is also one of the most important ingredients. He has to be able to oversee a situation in which players are moving around in a split second. The player has to control himself and wait a split second to give the cross. This is extremely difficult! The defensive pressure on this player and his speed are usually high. Still he has to remain calm when he delivers the cross. Finidi George was a master at this during his years at Ajax-Amsterdam. However, one of his successors, Tijani Babangida, was much too nervous during that deciding moment. His speed would be so high that he was not able to shift down a bit in the split second before he would give the cross. The overall result of his crosses were not good enough. This is, of course, very disturbing when it happens to an outside forward at Ajax. Another player who did master this extremely well was Brian Laudrup. It is a very important weapon when a player has feeling for giving the cross at the right moment when running at a high speed. Just think of the importance of the crosses given by Beckham while at world class Manchester United. To a certain degree, it is possible to train a player to give a good cross. A player such as Babangida will never master crossing the way Beckham is able to do it, however, he can improve the overall result of his crosses by practicing hard on this discipline. It is a matter of doing it over and over again, both individually and team tactically. This works the same way as it does for free kick and corner kick specialists, and playmakers in the midfield who practice crosses, long balls, give-and-goes and short passes.

▶ The opportunities of the outside attacker are best when the opponents lose possession while building-up. The double cover is then usually not in place yet. These are the situations where a team such as Ajax, with permanent outside attackers, can be very dangerous when the ball is played to one of them. When the outside attacker receives the ball when the build-up started in the back, then two defenders usually cover him and he can usually do nothing else but to just play it back, so the attack can be shifted somewhere else. When choosing to play with permanent outside attackers, you are very dependent on the qualities of these players, if they are on that day, and the way they are played the ball.

▶ During the build-up, a permanent outside attacker only has the use of a small 'corridor'. It is a team tactical guideline that he is supposed to stay on the outside and keep the field wide, as to create as much operational space in the center of the field as possible. These players need to possess specific qualities and plenty of team discipline to perform their tasks. An adequate youth football educational system creates the foundation for this.

▶ It is essential that an outside attacker is being supported by his teammates (defenders, midfielders and striker) on his build-up side of the field. This is again one of the many examples of team tactical coherence, to be able to play the positional game and the combination play as well as possible.

▶ Another good option for the outside attacker is to (team efficiently) switch positions with the striker. A good example of this is the way Johan Cruijff switched with his left forward.

▶ When observing outside attackers when the build-up is played on the other side of the field, too many times you can notice important shortcomings in their game; they are not actively involved. It is, for example, tactically difficult to mark an outside forward when he makes a run at the right moment towards the penalty box. To make it a surprising run demands good timing on the part of the attacker, a quality that he usually lacks. Furthermore, when the ball is crossed from the opposite side, he is usually too late in entering the penalty box.

- The outside attackers do not switch enough between coming into the ball and going deep. Or between going down the line and through the middle.
- When two defenders cover them, they too often choose to play the ball back instead of playing a more opportune long ball.
- When a team plays without permanent outside attackers, the operational space on the outside can be utilized by different players; central attackers, midfielders and outside defenders. Team tactically it is essential that these spaces are being used to the full width of the field during both the build-up and the attack. South American countries in particular sin against this team tactical rule. An example of this is the Colombian team during World Cup '94, when their opponents easily defended their one-dimensional attacking game through the center of the field.
- In the 4:4:2-team structure, several options are possible to attack over the flanks. The outside defenders play a large role in the attacking strategies of the Brazilian team. However, this demands that you have players with specific qualities. This type of player is developed within the Brazilian youth football system, just like the typical outside forwards are developed in the Dutch system. In the Italian 4:4:2 system, the outside midfielders utilize the space on the flanks, sometimes in correlation with the defenders. In the German system (5:3:2/3:5:2), this space is utilized by the outside 'defenders/midfielders'. You can already observe this in the German youth education system.
- However you look at it, it is important to develop set patterns with good team tactical coherence while playing over the flanks. The most space is found at the outsides of the field. However, even at the top-level, there are many teams who do not utilize this space enough. Just think of the battle Louis van Gaal had to engage in with world-class player Rivaldo while at Barcelona. Rivaldo has a nose for the goal and he prefers to play in and around the penalty box. He does not like to play as an outside attacker. In the team concept of the coach, he has to play in a different role, therefore his preference and the interests of the team collide. The coach is responsible for the interests of the team. Therefore a negative field of tension can develop.
- The attack over both the left and right flank has to be developed. To pass someone on the outside demands the development of specific qualities as a youth player. To be able to pass an opponent on the inside also demands tactical coherence in the use of the space by teammates. In any case, the overall result of attacking via the flanks is dependent on the technical-

tactical qualities needed to deliver a good cross. It is not
possible to train too much on this!

ATTACKS THROUGH THE CENTER

▶   The most efficient option when attacking through the center of
the field is to play a long ball to a forward who is sprinting deep.
The timing of both the 'passer' and the forward are essential.
We are talking about a window of opportunity that lasts a split
second, if you wait too long the advantage of the forward, who
starts his run, is gone or he is in an off-side position. During the
Olympic Games in the USA, the Brazilian team had a problem
scoring goals. A journalist asked Ronaldo what caused this
problem to occur. Ronaldo replied that when he went deep,
Giovanni, the player who had to give the long pass, held on to
the ball just a little too long. Giovanni enjoyed doing fancy
things while in possession of the ball, and therefore he let the
moment to pass the long ball - a window of opportunity that
lasts a split second -, usually go by. This situation occurs quite
often. Again and again it is about taking advantage of the
specific qualities of the striker, and adapting the build-up to him.
　　The efficiency of the striker does play an important role
in the result of the match. Due to the fact that the central
forward is the most tightly marked player, it is important that a
second player supports him. This player needs to be active
while moving in the correct position, and he needs to be strong
on the ball. He needs to operate in front of as well as behind
the striker. In other cases, it is the striker who is too eager to go
deep. He lacks the control to start his run at the correct
moment and is easily put in the offside position by the defensive
line: a lack of tactical insight in and oversight of the situation.
Especially in those situations when the ball is won in the build-
up or when the defensive line moves up, the striker must recognize the correct moment to go deep.

▶   Another option is the attack via the second central forward who
plays behind the striker. In most countries, this second forward
is usually an attacking midfielder. The combination of two
authentic forwards and an attacking midfielder has become
scarce. In the evolution of football this combination has, in the
view of most coaches, become an interfering factor in the
balance between the defense and the build-up/attack.

▶   There are two more options for the second (fake) forward. He
can, as the deep playing playmaker, function in the role of
'creator of the attack'. He is the target player who is played a

deep pass to his feet. Such a player has the technical and tactical qualities of a playmaker, however he operates in smaller spaces than the classical number 10 (attacking midfielder). He is a player who can dribble, give chip-passes, play give-and-goes and shoot on goal. These players are the best key players, just think of Baggio, Bergkamp, Zola, Zidane, Kanu etc. They are a valuable possession! This creator of the attack wants to receive the ball while coming toward the midfield. Furthermore, in all team structures, you need to have a deep striker, otherwise you are helping the defense by removing your most efficient weapon of attack.

- The other variation of the second forward is a player who correctly times his run and turns up deep. He does this in combination with the actions of the striker and the actions made via the flanks. In contrast with the function of the 'creator of the attack', the task of this player is to receive the ball behind the defense. This places high demands on recognizing the correct moment to sprint deep in combination with the actions made by the other attackers. Such players score goals on a regular basis because their actions surprise the defenders of the opponent.

- The attacks through the center can, of course, also be done by two central attackers who play next to each other. British teams in particular opt for this. This duo alternates between coming to the ball and going deep. This demands a longer period of development. It is important that the midfield supports these players, otherwise they become too isolated up front and they will have to rely too much on their individual actions. This assignment can become (too) tough considering the tight marking on these players. You can notice this while observing the two forwards of teams playing in the Italian league. This is one of the reasons why top English strikers fail to succeed in the Italian league. Performing while isolated with a defender marking you tightly at your back places high demands on how you control the ball and get past opponents.

- A dangerous attacking weapon, but tactically difficult to perform, is the give-and-go combination. Apart from the individual technical qualities of the 'giver' and the 'go-er', it is also impor-tant to recognize when to engage in a give-and-go combina-tion, when taking the total attacking context into account. The give-and-go combination is in training often used while shooting on goal. Mostly, however, it is then an isolated drill that has hardly any connection with the actual match reality. It is then an individual technical-tactical drill that is not recognized by the players in the more complex realistic match situation. To realize that goal, you will need to present the players   with training forms that will teach them to recognize, in a flash, when a situation asks for the playing of a give-and-go combination. The game ingredients, such as the position, the action of opponents, and the operational space, play a role in this. The individual qualities are also in this case the determining factor for the timing and the way the give-and-go combination is performed: to recognize the moment it should be played.

▸ An important tactical weapon can also be the involvement of the 'third man', who checks from the midfield to the player in possession on the wing. If he is successful or not depends on the moment he checks to the ball. If this 'third man' comes out of the defensive line, then he will be tough to defend. Just think of the role performed by Ronald Koeman or Danny Blind while playing at Ajax and in the Dutch national team.

ATTACKING GUIDELINES IN AND AROUND THE PENALTY BOX

Just as was the case for the give-and-go combination, the individual output also plays an important role with these guidelines. Besides recognizing the situation and the creativity of the players, their technical, mental and physical qualities are also of great importance.

Much too often after a well thought through and well performed build-up, you can observe that in the final attacking phase, the cross fails to reach its target. The player lacks individual class. A good action in this final phase demands a lot of individual work in training, otherwise the team tactical outcome is too small. The team tactical guidelines are also in place for the final phase, when playing in and around the penalty box. The outcome is most of all determined by the individual qualities.

The team tactical guidelines for the final phase are:
▸ Make sure there is an optimal force of players inside and around the penalty box. When the ball is crossed from the right flank, the left forward is often still too far away. As mentioned before: cutting inside towards the penalty box is too often also not performed.
While preparing for Euro '88, I instructed an assistant coach, Nol de Ruiter, to work with outside forward John van 't Schip and coach him when cutting to the inside. With the correct timing you can surprise your opponent. This timing is linked to the tactical insight into the situation at any given moment.
▸ An outside forward who is a good header - but also a defender or a midfielder in that position - is worth his weight in gold. This quality can be better developed than most people often think.

Sjaak Swart, the legendary right forward of Ajax, is living proof of this. Again, it is a matter of specialized individual training and the willingness to work on this aspect as a player.

▸ The teamwork between the central and the second forward is very important. Unfortunately, this is often not developed in great detail. This is also a piece of the team building process. The willingness of these forwards to gear their actions to one another, to serve the best interest of the team, is a difficult assignment for them. They both want to score goals themselves. However, it is all about playing as team efficiently as possible. Usually there is one forward that anticipates first and the second forward has to react to these actions immediately. This seems obvious and simple, but this is not true in real life. Too often, the individual interests of the forward prevail over the interests of the team. As a coach, you have to recognize this when it happens.

▸ The players in the second line, usually the midfielders, must quickly take up a position to be able to receive a pass being played back or to intercept a cleared ball.

▸ The third line functions as the cover defense and must stay involved and ready to act.

▸ Make sure you have guidelines in place for the second attacking phase that will go in effect when a cleared ball is intercepted. This is an important moment in the attack. Such a guideline is that the players again take up a new position very quickly in and around the penalty box. It is important that together they strive to take advantage of this newly developed attacking situation. The defense of the opponents is, after all, vulnerable at such a moment. A dangerous weapon in this situation is to play a deep pass to a player who is on the flank just inside the penalty box. This pass is hard to defend because the defender can easily commit a foul that can turn into a penalty kick. When the opponents clear a ball that is picked up by the other team, the forwards should in any case take up a position on the outsides of the penalty box. Another option is to play the ball to a player who is running into the space on the flanks or engage in a give-and-go combination with a forward inside the penalty box.

Another guideline is: 'never dribble unnecessarily into a wall of defenders.' If the ball is lost, the opponents will have an ideal situation to play the counter attack, because the players of the team that lost the ball will still be moving away from their own goal. When possession is lost in that situation, it will be deadly. So, when dealing with this wall of defenders, it is very important to act in a team efficient way. This is especially true for the man with the ball. However, he also needs to be supported by the alert team efficient actions of his teammates. This discipline also requires plenty of practice.

▶ The opposing defenders will try to pull the offside trap. It is often annoying to see how even top-notch players can kill dangerous looking attacks by not being alert enough in recognizing the offside trap. This can be understood when talking about central attackers, but there is no excuse for the outside attackers, who should have complete oversight of the situation. That it does happen too often is due to the fact that they are not alert enough in such game situations. They only have eyes for the ball and themselves. They do not notice the actions of the opponents.

Remark:

In this attacking phase, high demands are placed on the creative qualities of the individual players. However, guidelines are necessary to direct the complex traffic in the crowded penalty box, which ask for quick actions and reactions.

During the team tactical training sessions, it is obvious that the attacking patterns are linked to defensive patterns. Thus, we kill two birds with one stone.

Earlier on I mentioned that with attacking strategies you cannot lose sight of a healthy portion of opportunism. That choice will take care of the required surprise action and prevents, for example, circulation football becoming the goal in itself, instead of being a means. A style of play without opportunism will usually not be accepted by the crowd. It is too boring and sterile to watch. You can stimulate opportunism by giving it attention during the training sessions. Of course while playing match realistic games.

QUALITY OF THE INDIVIDUAL PLAYER

In conclusion: no matter how effective the performance of the team may be or how well the tasks, functions and strategies are executed, everything rises and falls with the individual qualities of the players. I can not repeat this enough. His technical, tactical, physical and mental baggage are the determining factors. This is a golden ground rule.

As a coach, you make an effort to develop an extra quality with each individual player: just a little bit more team efficiency. That little bit more is tedious work. An important prerequisite is that the coach and the player are both willing to bring the formulated guidelines to life while dealing with fewer or more game resistances.

Barcelona: a new challenge for the teambuilding process (1974)

The coach and his superstar (1976)

Naturally the positional games are fun to play and are useful for the coach while developing the individual technical-tactical qualities of players of any age (from 6-40 years old). However, the extra tactical development, the insight into the team tactical mechanism is a different story.

First of all, the coach must visually make clear which tactical guidelines are involved. Which players are (in)directly involved and how are they involved? Next, it must be translated to real training sessions, which come as close to the realistic match situation as possible. This requires that the complete group give all they have! This job is too difficult to just wing it. Whoever claims that he can succeed just on his intuition and experience either overrates himself or takes the easy way out.

The level of the coach can be noticed by the manner in which he inspires the players. That cannot be learned in a course. It is the individual quality of each coach, the personality of the coach. When the coach does not act in conformance to his personality, he will be in trouble. Any group of players will see through that.

When a player learns to look at the training sessions and the match through 'team glasses', and understands the use of team tactical training, the final step in becoming mature has been taken. The coach is fortunate when this occurs.

The assignment and challenge for every coach at whatever level is to get the maximum out of each player with the standard being the individual qualities of the player. It is pitiful that the evaluation of this, the critique and the power lays in the hands of others who have no insight into the matter. This is why coaches should pave their own roads and act according to their own views, without compromises. That being said, they should act with plenty of tact, lots of patience and with a feel for communication. And, hope for a bit of good luck!

The team building process is not the only important factor to achieve success. However, it does provide the team with a good dose of stability, so they are able to handle setbacks on and off the field. This optimally developed resistance against setbacks must be supported by a strong match mentality for each player.

The match mentality aspect is assembled from a range of match related mental qualities. These are patterned differently for each player, but are essential for every top-level player (and top-level athlete). The elements of match mentality are:

▶   Conviction and willingness to be a winner;
▶   Courage, self confidence and controlled fear to lose;
▶   Controlled aggressiveness, stamina and physical fitness;
▶   Ability to handle losing;
▶   Take and demand responsibility;
▶   Team discipline and team spirit;
▶   Responsibility for the team.

The match mentality is pliable and can be developed in nuances and patterns. Naturally, a ball virtuoso will not become a fighter in duels with the opponent. The controlled fear to lose also has its limits, a true goal scorer will not get thrown off balance by shooting a ball in the bleachers or when he misses a goal scoring opportunity. However, another player might be too scared to shoot or play the long ball. It is this solidarity and the effect players have on each other that will have a positive influence on their match mentality. To be responsible and feel responsible for achieving a collective performance is the most important tool for the coach to influence the individual match mentality.

The work atmosphere does play an important role in this. Positive and negative, internal and external occurrences influence the daily work atmosphere. Each and every occurrence, however innocent it may seem, has the potential to influence the team mentality and match mentality in a positive or less positive manner. It is obvious that every coach should always be alert to the atmosphere in his working environment. This is not an easy assignment, and there is no recipe for it. However the coach does not have to rely solely on his intuition. As with the team tactical process, there are also guidelines to structure this action. In the following chapter I will deal with this in more depth.

GUIDELINES FOR THE TEAM TACTICAL
TEAM BUILDING PROCESS:

ORGANIZATIONAL GUIDELINES
(FROM A TACTICAL POINT OF VIEW):
BASIC ORGANIZATIONAL FORMS
▶ 5:3:2, 4:4:2, 4:3:3 AND VARIATIONS THEREOF
▶ The choice is also determined by:
  - football history of a country;
  - tradition at the club;
  - views of the coach.

BASIC TASKS
THE BALANCE IN A TEAM
DEFENSIVE TEAM FUNCTION AS STARTING POINT FOR
THE BUILD UP AND ATTACK

STRATEGICAL TEAM TACTICAL GUIDELINES
FOR A PLAY MAKING STRATEGY
FOR A COUNTER ATTACK STRATEGY
PER TEAM FUNCTION
▶ **Defensive strategies**
  - formation

-    pressuring the opponent
-    positional play
-    offside
-    covering defense

▶ **Build-up strategies**
-    formation
-    circulation football
-    kick and run
-    opportunism

▶ **Attacking strategies**
-    attacks via the flanks
-    attacks through the center
-    guidelines for attacking in the final phase

Everything rises and falls with the quality of the individual player

CHAPTER 4

THE GROUND RULES OF THE PSYCHOLOGICAL TEAM BUILDING PROCESS

In the last chapter the central theme was the tactical team building process. This is something that happens mostly on the field. There is also a team building process that takes place off the field: the psychological or mental team building process. I would like to stress that these processes can be distinguished, but they cannot be separated.

Also, in the area of the psychological team building process, guidelines can be formulated, which make it possible to structuralize this process with the aim of gaining a clearer view of the situation. Just as with the team tactical team building process, these guidelines can act as a frame of reference and give you something to go on. The coach can decide which parts are useful to him.

In any case, this process demands constant attention. In top-level football it so happens there are constant forces at work from inside and outside the club, which can have a negative influence on the players and therefore on the team spirit. Often even little things, which might seem insignificant, can have disastrous consequences. A negatively tinted interview with the media, something that has been said in the player's lounge, an off the record comment made by the club's president or a small incident that occurred in training... Also the media can become an instant danger for the relations in the team or the relationship between a player and the coach. Continuous attention is required. The frame of reference contains the following points:

HARMONY

A coach can only function well if there is good harmony within the club and the team. The executive committee must show that they have full confidence in the coach. This is also true for the management. The executive committee and the co-workers (staff and management) and the head coach must form a tight group and present themselves as such to the outside world. If this does not happen, you can expect that problems will arise. When there is a situation of unity, there will be a work atmosphere of mutual respect and trust. For example, when the coach has the knowledge that when he disciplines a player, he will be supported.

The president, the manager and the coach must be in full agreement with each other. Not just when they are together, but especially also when they are among people from outside the club, the players, and the media. Only then will they have a binding effect on the team.

It is obvious that, especially in times when the club is not doing so well, you will be able to tell if there is true harmony in the club. It is in these situations that its effect will be the biggest.

Feyenoord-Rotterdam is a good example of a club that over the past few years has shown the importance of good harmony within a club. A few years ago, this club was on the edge of an athletic and financial precipice. The cause: the constant jurisdictional dispute between all parties within the club: board members, management and coaches. The media jumped all over this situation and the misery became increasingly larger. After Rob Baan was appointed as a (professional) board member in charge of technical affairs, and coach Leo Beenhakker was hired, peace and harmony returned to the club. The result was that the president more and more stopped making provoking remarks through the media. The work atmosphere gradually got better. A group of individuals was turned into a cohesive team that was willing to work for and with each other. The coach was able to better influence the team tactically, the manager had a nose for good players, and notice what happened: Feyenoord won the championship again.

There are also plenty of examples on international football scene. Just look at German clubs such as Schalke 04, Borussia Dortmund and Bayern Munich. For several years these clubs suffered bad results due to a power struggle between the president and manager on one side and the coach on the other side. The result was constant conflicts and disappointing results. One coach after the other was fired. The turn-around occurred at these clubs because the internal disputes were settled and the executive committee and management did not panic when the results were disappointing. Consequently, the door to success in international football competitions opened up. When a club changes its coaching staff too many times an opportune style of play will be the result. A coach must have enough time to get his points across to the team. A successful team building process does take time.

Another example is Real Madrid. Countless millions have been invested in players, but for many years coaches were not given a chance to create a team out of them, and to set out a long-term policy. Guus Hiddink was appointed coach after a successful World Cup in 1998. He was brought in as the savior and received the assignment to contract younger players. He won the World Championship for club teams, but when he seriously planned to cut some players, forces in the background started to emerge. The executive committee at Real Madrid was in this situation also susceptible to this, and Guus Hiddink was, just as many coaches that preceded him, forced to leave. You will have to pay the price when pursuing such a policy.

The president of FC Barcelona deserves much more admiration. The results in the Spanish competition were quite disastrous during Louis van Gaal's first weeks at the helm of Barcelona. The pressure not only from the outside world, but also from the executive committee to take action was mounting on a weekly basis. However, Nunez kept supporting Louis van Gaal. Herewith the foundation was laid for the latter successes. A good president, who firstly serves the interests of the club, is worth his weight in gold. When he is also able to select a good coach, then he deserves a statue.

A president who is too ambitious can be a disturbing factor when striving for harmony. A president is important for a club when it comes to external contacts with sponsors, organizations, institutions, and politicians. He carries with him the ultimate responsibility concerning this area. He is also responsible for the organization within the club, but often he will delegate this to the management team of the club. However, a president should not get involved in football technical manners. The coach carries the ultimate responsibility for this area. When the president makes remarks about technical aspects it will definitely create havoc. This is also true when a president gives a speech to the team in a time when the results are disappointing. This will almost always be explained as a sign of a lack of confidence towards the coach. This train of rumors will be difficult to stop.

MEDICAL STAFF

During important international tournaments, people and occurrences from outside the group can have a negative influence on the harmony. Famous are the discussions about the medical care for the national team players during European and World Championships. During tournaments with such big interests, the players of course wish to recuperate as soon as possible when they get injured or have other discomforts. Some of these players prefer to consult with their personal physical therapists.

During Euro '88 in Germany, I was confronted with this exact situation. Quite a few players were treated by a haptonomist (a specialized massage therapist). They asked me if he was allowed to treat them while in training camp. Naturally, I first consulted with the team physician, Frits Kessel. He was not pleased with this request, because he was convinced that this would be explained by the media as distrust towards the KNVB medical staff. I shared this concern, because this therapist enjoyed the spotlight a little bit too much.

I explained this to the players who had made the request. However, because it is also in the best interest of the coach that players feel that they have done all that is in their power to be physically and mentally fit, I agreed to these treatments at a location outside the hotel.

It is of great importance that you pick up such signals from the players at an early stage and communicate with the players involved. Personal interests need to take a back seat when trying to reach the most optimal performance level possible. To achieve this, it is essential to have harmony within the group, especially when you are in a situation where the media has an insatiable hunger for news items.

COLUMNS

A threat to the harmony in a group during such tournaments can be the columns written by star players for newspapers and weekly magazines. You can not forbid them to write the columns. The players make a lot of money writing them, and each player has the personal freedom to choose to write columns.

Beforehand, I do point out the incompatible benefits and interests. Both the team and the coach benefit from the tranquility surrounding the team. On the other hand, the media loves disturbances. This is why the media almost always support the individual players, because then they do not have to take the interests of the team into account. You cannot blame them for this, because it is easiest to score with an article when the times are turbulent. Journalists often are hunters searching for news that can be made more spectacular. In almost all cases they can find someone to do their dirty work. The danger of losing the tranquility will then start knocking on the gates of the club. Right away the harmony in the team is in jeopardy.

During a European or World Championship of course, the player does not write the column himself. He has to depend on what the 'ghost writer' does with his comments. The player must assess this well beforehand. Furthermore, these players should not be allowed to voice criticism of teammates, the tactics used in the match or about the coach in these articles. The balance between the individual and the team interests is at stake here.

CHARACTER

The chance that disturbances occur within the team is bigger in the Netherlands than in for example Spain and Italy. Those players have a bigger acceptance of what the coach demands of them compared to Dutch players. As with an abundance of people from the Netherlands, these players are also quick to voice their opinion. The media like to take advantage of this. However, this feature can be a positive influence on the team tactical team building process. Dutch players who dare to voice their opinions are often creative on the field. They take initiative and try to find solutions.

Let's return to the harmony within a club. In any case, the aim must be to strive for the optimal willingness, attitude, and motivation of players, staff and the executive committee to keep the work atmosphere as positive as possible. Also, the football related aim could function as the common 'dream', for example; not getting relegated, to qualify for the Champions League, or to finish in the top 5 of the table, etc. What matters is the common short term and long term goal. An invaluable binding agent is the long-term vision related to football affairs. This is the guideline for the youth education system, the style of play, and the code of conduct, and needs to be monitored through the years. Even the concept 'guarding the culture of the club' plays a role in this. This is not a simple task in a work atmosphere in which opportunism and unpredictability play an important role. Therefore, it is necessary that all areas of the work force support a vision.

RULES OF CONDUCT FOR BOTH ON AND OFF THE FIELD

Rules of conduct are necessary to have correct mutual relationships. An important ground rule is: do not critique teammates, the coach, the executive committee or the tactics used to anyone who falls outside the immediate team structure. Within the team structure there should be as much opportunity to communicate as possible. Rules concerning the meals, the tidying up of different things, being on time for practice, when leaving on a road trip or at meetings are also important. In short, a set of guidelines with the main aim of creating a feeling of belonging to the team, and team discipline. Such rules of conduct for both on and off the field only make sense if they are being enforced, not only by the coach, but also by the players themselves.
You should strive that the captain or other key players within the team enforce these agreements and give the right example themselves. This works much better than the coach constantly having to enforce the rules.

By giving some examples from my long career as a coach, I will try to make clear how I dealt with enforcing these rules of conduct.

CRITIQUE

The KNVB had put a lot of pressure on me to become the national team coach gearing up for Euro '92 in Sweden. Eventually I gave in at the expense of a 'safer' position as a member of the board. This difficult job started with a friendly game on the road. At the airport in Amsterdam, I made clear to all the players that success would only be possible if we had a good atmosphere in the team. After the fiasco during World Cup '90 in Italy, an elaborate explanation was not necessary. This fiasco could largely be blamed on a lack of harmony, lack of mutual respect, and cliques within the team.

Negative comments in the media were a direct threat. I forbade the players to critique teammates, the coach, or the tactics used via the media. However, they were of course allowed to critique their own performance...

Not long after this, I read an article in which Ronald Koeman criticized the tactics used by the national team. In itself this critique was mild, but it was against the agreed on team policy. I sent him a fax in which I explained to him that this interview would have consequences. Especially as one of the team leaders, he should have known and sensed that these comments were inappropriate and made at an undesirable moment. I pointed out to him that in the best interest of the team, I had to act and suspend him for one match.

As a coach, you have to be lucky that a key player has broken a rule and can be disciplined for this. When the 18th player breaks a rule, it has no impact on the psychological team building process. The attention that this suspension received in the media had the desired effect.

Recently, I talked to Koeman about this incident. He can understand this suspension because he is now a coach himself. When it actually happened of course, he did not. As a coach, you cannot lose a night's sleep over this. You have to act in the best interest of the team, also for the long term. Players do not realize enough, usually unintentionally, the results of voicing their opinions.

AGREEMENTS

Ronald Koeman still has a problem with a solution I came up with for a different problem. We were in a training camp preparing for Euro '88 in Germany. Due to the fact that the season is so long in Spain, Barcelona still had matches left to play. There were still matches scheduled that were important for the championship. The coach at Barcelona at that time was Dutchman Johan Cruijff. He called me with the request to give Ronald Koeman time so he could play in an important league match. I replied that I would honour his request, however I would only agree to this one match. I of course had to keep the interests of the national team in mind.

When Ronald Koeman returned to the training camp, he asked if it was all right to leave to go to Barcelona once more to play in a testimonial match. I did not appreciate this coming from Johan Cruijff. He should have told Koeman 'a deal is a deal'. I can still remember having the meeting with Ronald Koeman where I told him that he could depart to Barcelona, however, if he choose to do this then I would definitely choose to play Danny Blind instead of him. And, not just for the final preparation match against France, but also for the matches during the European Championships. Koeman was very disappointed, he even asked captain Ruud Gullit and 2nd captain Marco van Basten to talk to me and to try to change my mind. Given the situation I did not feel that this would be called for. It had nothing to do with my feeling that Koeman was not deserving of this testimonial match, although he felt that was the reason. At that period in the preparations, I was obligated to put the interests of the team before the interests of an individual player.

I said it before: Ronald Koeman still has problems with the decision I made. Maybe this will change when as a top-level coach he is confronted with a similar situation...

In any case, this is a typical situation of a player who thinks on the basis of his own ideas and interests, in contrast to a coach who is obligated to take the side of the team and to set and guard the rules of conduct for both on and off the field. We have not even started to take into account the interests of Danny Blind in this example.

Every coach has to decide how he is going to guard the correct balance between the interests of the team and the interests of the individual. This is often a delicate game. During the 1999-2000 season, Ruud Gullit fell victim to this while coaching at Newcastle United. In any case, it is a must to communicate. It is difficult for any person to ignore his own self-interests. We can usually see the necessity for others to do this, just not ourselves! There are guidelines for this, but there are not ready made solutions. Every situation is just a little bit different.

FINES

The next two examples are also very recognizable. During one of my early years at Ajax-Amsterdam, a well-known player arrived too late. I gave him a substantial fine. The amount of the fine is not important. However the signal give is; the rule that you should be on time counts for everyone. This player did not accept the fact that he was fined and threatened to take this to the executive committee. I then told him that I would be saddened if he took this step, but that I could not stop him from doing it. That was all I said. The next day there was an article in the newspaper about this incident. Such a small incident is instantly blown out of proportion. Another day later, the player changed his mind and the whole incident was resolved. This could have ended differently. An incident like this proves that such a conflict should preferably be solved in private. However, even the walls have ears in top-level athletics.

During the World Cup of 1974, another such possibility presented itself. A team leader got caught going out to a bar, breaking a team rule. I used this incident as a binding agent for the group. I called all the players in for a meeting and asked the player involved to wait outside until a decision had been made regarding if he was allowed to stay. I told the team that I refused to act as a police officer during this tournament and that I would have no problem if this player was removed from the team. I told them that I would like to consult them, because cutting this player would have far reaching consequences for the complete group due to his key role in the team. In the end the group decided to give this player, who had to wait in the hallway like a small child, one more chance. The responsibility to come to this decision immediately put a positive pressure on the group to stick to the team rules. This was the aim of this meeting. Again, I was lucky that it concerned an important player, so this approach had the desired effect. As a result, this incident did not leak to the media... This is a positive sign that the solidarity in the team is good.

THE TEAM HIERARCHY

The stronger the personality of the coach, the easier it is for him to influence the hierarchy within the team. When you are the type of coach who does not naturally stand above the players, then you have to hope that a few key players positively influence the pecking order in the team.

Football players know that there is a certain ranking within the team. The players who are at the bottom of the ladder usually will accept this. The coach has to be alert to those players who are almost at the top of the hierarchy. For them there will always come a day that they feel it is their turn to be on top of the food chain! You have to keep a close eye on this process, and you have to ask yourself if that moment is actually there or not. If it is not, you will have to act swiftly to prevent big problems from occurring. The ranking in the team is not a constant factor! The athletes themselves have a need for natural team leaders. They demand that the coach follow this process closely. That the consequences can be drastic if the coach acts too late was obvious during Euro '96 in England. Edgar Davids and Clarence Seedorf did not accept the ranking order in the Dutch national team anymore. This behavior was the source of the forming of cliques in the team. Coach Hiddink acted by sending Davids home. This was the most drastic measure that could have been taken. However, when you have to make this decision, it is usually too late and too much has already occurred. Such a process cannot be prevented anymore due to the role of the media. I was not part of the staff at that time, so it is hard for me to say if this could have been handled in a different way. However, I am a proponent of dealing with such problems in the privacy of the people involved. Then, there is always the possibility of coming up with alternative solutions. Of course this is not always possible, and the coach will then play a losing match.

When you pay close attention to details, you can recognize the existence of such a conflict when watching the game. Some players will not play to the service of other players, they do not make the runs they usually make, and they neglect their basic task just a little sooner than normal. Outside the field this process produces small irritations, which have a negative influence on the atmosphere in the team. In addition, this incident was blown out of proportion by the media, due to the fact that they made it a racial issue. Such a case will then grow uncontrollably. There is no use in denying that there is no truth to any of it. The media will jump on a case like this because they need something interesting to write about on a daily basis during such a championship.

Another example of problems that arose because the hierarchy in a team was not accepted occurred during the preparation of the Dutch national team for the world championships of 1990 in Italy. A number of incidents followed one another. First of all, the players announced that they had no confidence in the capabilities of their coach, Thijs Libregts, to lead them during the World Cup. Ruud Gullit was their spokesman. This put the KNVB in a difficult position. Should they support their coach or suspend some key players? When this happens, the actual practice has taught us that this creates an impossible working environment for the coach. However, the coach did not accept his dismissal (which was unparalleled in history) and took this matter to the courts. The judge appropriately wanted to know how many players had lost confidence in the coach. This forced the KNVB to call in all the national team players, including those playing abroad, to hold a meeting where the votes would be counted. This was to weird to be true. This farce took place at the national airport in Amsterdam. This caused an even bigger division within the team, because the players did not want to believe that they had no other option but to comply with the judge's orders. The players felt that the KNVB shirked their responsibility. This scenario only produces losers; Thijs Libregts, the players, the KNVB, and above all a ruined atmosphere for the successor.

This was not the end of the story. The AC Milan players, Gullit, Rijkaard and Van Basten definitely wanted Johan Cruijff to be the successor. In the meantime, the time had arrived that the team should start to prepare for the tournament. The coach of Ajax-Amsterdam, main supplier of players of the national team, at that time was Leo Beenhakker. Although he was the second choice behind Johan Cruijff, the executive committee of the KNVB, of which I myself was a member, decided to offer the coaching position to Beenhakker because the program had to be started in a very short time. It was obvious that it was a 'mission impossible'. After all that had happened, he did not succeed in making up the differences of opinion within the team. Due to this fact, the national team of 1990 did not by far reach its highest possible level of performance. The match and team mentality were not optimal, which is a prerequisite for performing well at such a world class tournament.

A totally different approach: the role played by Vanenburg during his final years at PSV-Eindhoven is an example of not taking the natural hierarchy within the team into account. It comes natural to a player to be a team leader on and off the field. It did not fall within the character of Vanenburg to be a team leader. However, the staff at PSV wished for him to play this role. The final result: Vanenburg, his teammates, and the staff were all frustrated.

An example from my own coaching experience: This incident occurred during the qualifying phase for the European Championships of 1988. We could qualify for the tournament in our final match in and against Greece. Our captain came to the training camp with an injury. However, when the match day arrived he felt fit to play. You could feel the tension in the locker room before the match. As a coach you are happy when the warm-up starts, so the tension can be released.

Ten minutes before the game when we get back into the locker room, the captain announces that he is too injured to start the match. At that moment, this was an enormous set back for the team. You could tell by looking at the faces of the players. I ranted and raged at this player, and told him that he could no longer be the team captain. This was maybe not a proper response. However, yhou use such an incident as a binding agent for those players who will start the match. That is what you use a player for at that moment. I do not regret that I did this. At this level, at such a crucial moment, I felt that the end justified the means.

I did, however, make a different mistake at that moment. The captain remained all by himself, as a wounded animal, in the locker room. Of course, he became a grateful victim of the media. I should have at least had a staff member or a board member keep the media out of the locker room. Another experience to learn from...

That even the captain of a national team can make a mistake proves again that you constantly have to focus the attitude and the behaviour of players toward teamwork. Players have a natural tendency to think from what is best for them individually. It is difficult for a player to take the best interest of the team into account, when it is at the expense of his own interest. When it concerns other players, they of course agree that they should take the interest of the team into account.

This is of course not only true for football players. There is talk of an incident that occurred when Timmer, an executive of multinational Philips who was hired to put the company's affairs in order, went to the airport where several managers were getting ready to depart for a business trip to a faraway destination. He asked them if it would not have been possible to make the deals by phone instead of making this long trip. It is not for everyone to turn down an attractive trip, and take the best interest of the company into account. In the overall picture, this may seem to be a futility. What does matter is the attitude of the people concerned and not so much the incident itself.

During the crisis period that occurred at Philips, Mr. Timmer spent a lot of time and effort on team building. Team meetings were held on a daily basis. Especially in the business world, the mental team building process plays a dominant role. In athletics it serves as an invaluable prerequisite to realise the team tactical team building process. This does not play as big a role in the business world. Within a company there is just not a direct confrontation between two parties. Above all, it is the correct work attitude that is important. The psychological aspect.

KINGDOMS

As said earlier: 'every player feels like he is a kingdom onto himself'. One player more than the other, and the star players usually the most. It is a major task of the coach to unite these 'kingdoms' so as to create a forceful team. Every player wants to shine in a way that is best for him. This is normal human behavior, but in a team setting, the individual is of minor importance to the team, the interests of the team and success. Players may shine, but only in the best interest of the team. This will go smoothly, as long as there is success. When it threatens to go wrong, players have the tendency to save their own image. At Barcelona, where there is plenty of press who are critical of everyone and everything, I learned to recognize this behavior of players as panic attacks. Those players who were most susceptible to this behavior started to play more and more for themselves. The team discipline, the invaluable basis for executing their team task and team function diminished. Therefore the performance level went down noticeably.

I profited from this once while coaching at 1. FC Köln. We lost 0-1 at home against Barcelona in a UEFA Cup match. Nobody thought we would have a shot at reaching the next round. Before the match at Barcelona, I spoke to the team about us having a chance if we would score the first goal. I knew from my experience at Barcelona, that if that would happen, the Barcelona players would get nervous and start neglecting their basic tasks.

You have to have the good fortune in such a match that Barcelona does not finish their chances early on in the match. After 15 minutes it could have been 2-0 for Barcelona, but we scored from a counter attack and the scenario I predicted came true. Their organization on the field was gone and we beat Barcelona 1-4.

CLEAR OBJECTIVES

Every coach needs to have the skill to formulate realistic and challenging objectives that are appealing to the players.   They provide insight to all parties involved. Clear objectives are a binding agent for the team.

In the team tactical team building process, I have already described how I confronted the Dutch national team of 1974, who were in preparation for the World Cup, with a new and adventurous concept. When the complete team supported this attacking concept, this objective became the perfect binding agent. I could only afford to introduce this new concept in our playing style because I had the use of a unique group of players. Otherwise this objective would not have been realistic, and would have had a contrary effect.

It was clear to me in 1988 that we had great individual players. This new generation of football players, Van Basten, Gullit, and Koeman, had to hear over and over again that they were good players, but that they were still not as good as the World Cup team of 1974 with Cruijff, and others. You can then use this as a binding agent. You keep telling the group that here in Germany, where the previous generation lost the championship game 14 years ago, it is possible to win the title with good football.

Next to team objectives, most coaches also formulate objectives for individual players. Coach Foppe de Haan does this at his club Heerenveen. Just as in the corporate world, he does this at the start of the season, and he holds evaluation talks with the players. Amongst other things, players write down what they want to improve on tactically and technically this season and what their individual objectives are.

COMMON ENEMY

During the psychological team building process the coach can use the 'common-enemy-approach' as a binding agent for the team. A very well known situation occurred during the successful European championships of 1988, when the team and myself, very deliberately, reacted against the board members of the Football Association of the Netherlands. This was not very proper behavior on my part, but the board members obviously put their personal interests above those of the team. I tried to use this fact to our advantage, necessity knows no law.

This episode started during the qualification stage for Euro '88, in 1986. During that time I was the technical director for the KNVB and not the national team coach. This was a deliberate choice, I felt that I had done my share as a coach at that level, and I had the desire to work on creating a long-term policy. However, in no time at all, problems arose. First Kees Rijvers stepped down as coach and his successor Leo Beenhakker felt that after one year he did not receive the appropriate backing from the executive committee. The renewal of his contract was being put off time after time. Looking back on this, he probably felt blessed because this gave him the opportunity to accept an offer from Real Madrid to become the new coach.

The result was that we did not have a coach again, and I decided to take the job myself. However, something peculiar was going on. Several people informed me that a member of the executive committee of the KNVB, who was sitting in the VIP section of the stadium, did not enjoy the success of the national team. He was of the opinion that Johan Cruijff, the club coach of most of the players, should have a say in the technical football affairs of the national team. As a result, the good performances of the team did not sit well with this executive committee member. It might seem like an unbelievable story line, but it truly happened! There is even more to this story: the newspapers would write about national team players who had to be re-taught how to play football again when returning to Ajax after spending time with the national team under my guidance.

I then went to visit the chairman of the KNVB, informed him about the ridiculous situation that was happening and turned in my resignation. I did not want to, and could not work anymore under these circumstances. Eventually I received the ok to leave if I put up a 450.000 guilder compensation fee. The executive committee was convinced that an offer from PSV-Eindhoven was the reason for my resignation. I stayed on after having meetings with the KNVB. In the final meeting, I was asked by a board member if I was still motivated enough to lead the team at Euro '88. Well, if there was ever someone motivated to do well, it was me at that particular moment! I did inform them that I would be leaving directly after the tournament was over.

I started the preparations for the tournament with mixed feelings toward some board members. That in itself created a field of tension.

This story was to be continued at the tournament. First of all, I had to meet on a daily basis with Chairman Jacques Hogewoning about all that was happening around the national team. I have already explained my reasoning why chairman should not interfere with football technical affairs. I found this to be a very difficult assignment. I then told the chairman that 'I would have no time during the day and that he had no time for this at night, so all there was left was the early morning before breakfast...' I met just once with this chairman and after that this 'problem' had solved itself. He could not muster having to meet with me at 8 o'clock in the morning after having a tough evening.

It was harder for me to react to three other situations that occurred, because they endangered the direct interests of the team. More strongly put: I still get mad just thinking about it.
It started with the chaos around the complimentary tickets for the players. One player got a whole stack while another did not get any. Talk about stirring up trouble...

There was also a proposition from the executive committee to have the players, after the match, wait in a neutral area until it was time to embark on the trip back to the hotel. I found that to be an excellent idea. You always have to wait for players who have to get tested for performance enhancing drugs and this would be an opportunity for the other players to meet with their family members. However, what happened? The executive committee was using us. The room quickly filled with sponsors and media who would stampede the players. I then announced that we would not go to this 'neutral' area anymore, but go back to the hotel at our own leisure. The players backed me on this. There is yet another story to prove that the executive committee played a dirty game in 1988, instead of supporting the quest of the national team. This happened before the opening match of the tournament against Russia. It was about a 30-minute drive from the hotel to the stadium while being escorted by the police.

It started out all right, the players love such a police escort. It creates a bit of positive aggression, which is a good atmosphere to have before a match. However, the bus driver failed to take a known short cut, but instead took the most crowded route through the center of the town. Unbelievable! After sitting in this bus for an hour and a half the atmosphere changes. We are talking about arriving too late for the opening match of the European Championship.

In the end, we drove against traffic and took a different route to the stadium. In retrospect, it became clear what had happened. The bus driver had been given the assignment to drive past a hotel where a reception was held for the executive committee of the KNVB and the sponsors. This hotel has a large balcony and when the bus would pass, the board members and the sponsors could then wave at the bus... From that moment on, I decided to declare the board members as 'common' enemies of the team and make a binding agent out of them. Sometimes the media are also 'misused' to achieve this objective. An example of this is the dumping in the water of a journalist from a Dutch national newspaper during World Cup '74. In the eyes of the players and the staff, he was too critical. The Italian team took this a step further during World Cup '82, and declared a total media boycott...

The 'us, as a team, against the angry world outside'-idea can be used at any level. It is a prerequisite however, that the coach, staff, and players all feel the same way.

It is funny that I myself have been used as a common enemy. This occurred during World Cup 1990, in Italy. It was not as a coach, but as a board member, in charge of technical affairs involved with the national team. This was the reason that I was present at each training session. There was tension in the team from the beginning, and due to the disappointing results the atmosphere was not getting any better. Obviously comparisons are being made with successful tournaments, such as Euro '88. After a disastrous match against Egypt (1-1) in Palermo, and a shiftless attitude of several players during practice, coach Beenhakker retreated with his team to a locker room to escape from a threatening lightning storm. He closed the locker room door in dramatic fashion and embarked on a verbal storm. A historic thunderous speech followed in the ultimate attempt to save what could be saved. Afterwards I heard from players that the coach had stressed to say farewell to the Euro '88-syndrome, and especially to the spirit of Michels. I am writing this in a nicer way than the actual words that came out of Beenhakker's mouth during this speech. When putting myself in his shoes, I can even understand why he did this. When putting this in the correct perspective, you would understand that it had nothing to do with lack of respect. It was a desperate attempt of Beenhakker to create unity within the team. A coach may and must do this. However, he should have told me about what happened himself.

CULTURE OF THE CLUB

In the psychological team building process the culture of the club plays an important role. The culture of a club is the overall vision of the club. This vision is supported by everyone in the club, from players to staff to the chairman. An example could be that everyone realizes that if they are to stay with the club they will have to respect certain rules. Every club accentuates different areas. This is fine as long as the culture of the club remains recognizable.

At Real Madrid, every player knew that they would be dismissed if they ever attacked the club in public. This was true for both the substitutes and the star-players. However these same players knew that they could always count on the club in times of trouble, even after they had stopped playing.

In the Netherlands, Ajax-Amsterdam is a very well known club with a strong culture. The culture at Ajax is recognizable through their style of play, which is a result of their team building process. Every player, from an under-10, up to the striker of the first team, knows what is expected of him when playing for Ajax. This creates a strong binding agent in the club. The more extreme and recognizable the culture in the club, the better it works.

In the culture of Ajax, the feeling of being one big family is an important aspect of the club. Such a strong culture will help the club survive in times of trouble. The club is more resistant to negative factors and the management and the executive committee will not get agitated as quickly. Nobody hangs the club's dirty laundry outside. This is only possible when key individuals within the club repeatedly speak the same convincing language.

A basic question in a good team building climate is: what is the culture in our club? Which basic principles and basic agreements are important to us? Such a climate creates a trustworthy feeling and mutual respect by all involved. However, this does not guarantee that it could never go wrong. This is just one of the team building aspects. It does take care of a consequent policy within the club. When times are rough, and every club goes through such a period, this creates the best guarantee to survive as a 'family'. There are many known positive and negative examples of this.

STRATEGY OF CONFRONTATION

Within the mental team building process I sometimes deliberately chose to use a strategy of confrontation. This has nothing to do with lack of respect, I sometimes chose to use it in the best interest of the team. The objective was to create a field of tension and improve the team spirit.

There are no rules for the use of this strategy of confrontation. In any case, do not use it just because some other coaches got results with it. Most of all, the creation of conflict situations reflects on the personality and position of the coach. As is true for many things, if you use the strategy of confrontation but are not the type of coach who would normally use it, then you can only fail. A democratic coach can do well with a team, especially when he has two or three players on the field who arrange everything for him. When you are such a type of coach, do not force yourself to be an authoritarian. If the strategy of confrontation does fit with your personality, then use it with your best players. It does not make any sense to use it with substitute players or weaker players on the team. This won't help in creating a focussed team. It just creates problems.

Dealing with key players (I would rather not use the term star-players) is essential in the team building process. These players not only excel individually, but they are also strong in the team tactical aspect. Save yourself the trouble of trying out new things when key players do not side with you on this. The players with a supporting role are not recognized as team leaders and they do not come around to do the things that are important for the team. Then, only a small incident is needed to send onto the field a team that is afraid to lose. Next, the team rules are not being supported anymore and the team spirit loses its power. Players then fall back on their individual game and the performance level drops.

THE CREDIBILITY OF THE COACH

Team building can only be successful when the coach is credible as an expert in football affairs. He must be genuine, and be capable through didactical steps to transfer his vision to the players and be able to formulate realistic objectives.

The coach's own football background and career as a coach do play a role. When he has trained and played at the top level, he will more quickly be able to recognize what occurs in the match. However, it is necessary in modern day top-level football that this invaluable experience is supported by a structural theoretical knowledge of football and training. He has to have gone through adequate coaching educational training. He will then become a football personality who has faith in himself and is capable of transferring his knowledge and experience to the team.

Furthermore, he must be able to function as the leader of the team under all circumstances. Even under the highest pressure, the coach must be immune to stress and be able to handle bad results, protesting fans, rebelling substitutes, harsh criticism from the media or a demanding executive committee. The impact of football as the number 1 sport in the world can not be underestimated. When the behavior of the coach becomes inundated with fear and is constrained, very shortly his credibility will be affected.

By the way, it is not a necessity that a top-level coach has a history of being a top-level player. Sometimes this might even be a negative factor, because it is hard for a former star player to empathize with players who do not possess all the same qualities. Sometimes they also lack the required leadership qualities.

At the world class level an additional quality is required. The Germans call it 'fingerspitzengefühl'. It means intuitively knowing where the (football) shoe pinches. This cannot be learned at any coaching course. To be capable of reaching the absolute world class level, a coach must have gone through an extended experience as a top-level player. Such a coach has experienced all there is to know. This gives him acting-knowledge that cannot and should not be taught at the coaching courses. The coaching courses should teach other qualities: for example how to function as a leader of a group, and to master all the aspects of the training mechanism. And also, to learn how to structure the invaluable (practical) acting-knowledge, with the objective to teach others how to become better players, both individually as well as for the team. And, learning to manage football technical aspects, media relations, etcetera, etcetera.

In the Netherlands, there were many discussions about offering the position of national team coach to former top-level player Frank Rijkaard, who had just finished his coaching education program. The circumstances were to his advantage. He could profit from his extended experience as a world-class player. He followed the excelled coaching course for former professionals with great results. Frank attracted attention not just because of his expert and keen match analyses. Also, his internship at professional club FC Utrecht produced nothing but positive feedback. An important factor was that he had no doubt that he was able to take on this difficult job - reaching the optimal result during Euro 2000, which would be held in the Netherlands - and that he would succeed.

His disadvantage was that he had lacked experience as a coach at the top-level. I believe that he should not have taken the job if the Netherlands had to play qualification matches. Then the time period would have been too short. Now he was able to gain the experience needed in the year and a half gearing up to the tournament. He could experiment and learn from his mistakes while the pressure to achieve results was minimal. During this time frame, he could fall back on knowledgeable colleagues at the KNVB. This is the reason I believed he could succeed, especially when taking his strong personality into account. Looking back on Euro 2000, it is clear that Rijkaard's 'fingerspitzengefühl' was well developed.

CONSULT SITUATION

When a coach has confidence in his capabilities, he will then not shy away from situations where players are being consulted. It is then two-way traffic: give advice and be given advice, to take responsibility and to give responsibility. Because of this, the involvement of the players in reaching the objectives will be enlarged. However, precaution is needed. Only the top players within the hierarchy of the team qualify to take part. However, even then it remains to be seen if the team leader is football tactically adept enough to be able to contribute to the discussions. Sometimes as the coach you have to put oil on the fire of the discussion, but must never allow the flames to burn out of control.

COMMUNICATION

Team building rises and falls with good communication: thé resource and the correct attitude to perfect the team building. Through the proper form of communication, everyone knows what is expected of him.

Every training session is a form of communication. Players have the right to know what the objective of a training exercise is and what role they play in it. The cook (coach) determines which ingredients he will use in the menu of football training, in a way that his clientele (the players) enjoy consuming it. Every cook processes the ingredients in a different manner. That is the way it should be. However, the basic rules are the same for everyone.

Communication and enjoyment (a positive experience) will yield the best result. Your clientele will gladly return and will be open to making the team tactical problems their problems and working to improve them on the field. This is the ultimate attainable feat. When a coach has achieved this, then he deserves to be named 'master chef'.

The coach does need to have a feel for what he says to whom and when. The multi-national make-up of the current teams does not make it easy for the coach to deal with this. Language problems can create a murmur in the background, on the field as well as outside the field. Above all, the coach needs to take the cultural background of the individual players into account when communicating with them. For example, it does not bother players from the Netherlands when the coach criticizes them in front of the group. During the scrimmages, the players will keep their slacking colleagues focussed by attacking them verbally and physically. Players who are brought up in a different culture might find this to be a humiliating experience. A coach of a multi national team has a difficult job ahead of him when considering the team building process. A lot depends on the correct attitude of the players. Where there's a will, there's a way.

TRAINING CAMPS

PRE-SEASON CAMPS

Training camps can be an important aid for the team building process outside the field. For example during pre-season. When starting to work with a new group, these atmosphere positive training camps can be of value. Furthermore, you have several training sessions a day in which you can structurally work on team tactical aspects.

The so-called 'mentality camps', for example survival camps in the woods, have no value to the team tactical process. They are better suited for business groups, who are searching for activities in which the accent is put on working together. For football players who work closely together on a daily basis, this objective is reached through different means. This is why they should spend their valuable time on the team tactical team building process.

BEFORE MATCHES

The training camps held before matches are a different story. These are more frequently held abroad in comparison to the Netherlands. This is very logical when taking into account that the Netherlands is relatively small. We are able to drive to each stadium when leaving the same day. Also, the attention of the media for most matches is nothing in comparison to the media craziness as seen in the big football countries.

Furthermore, most players from the Netherlands are fairly level-headed. They would rather prepare for the next match in the familiar surroundings of their homes. Training camps as a preparation for regular league matches are an exception to the rule. This creates a special situation when a team embarks on a training camp before a league match.

Before a match, every player feels insecure in some fashion or another. It does not matter how much self-confidence he has. As a reaction to this, he searches for certain securities. This can be found in artists and athletes alike, when considering their superstitions. A coach must realize that these securities can be found while preparing for a match in familiar surroundings.

When travelling with a club such as Barcelona, you stay in the nicest hotels in the world. However, when I was the coach, when preparing for a home match we would stay in a modest hotel. The food was good, but I cannot begin to imagine that this hotel had even one star. However, it would have been a mistake if I had chosen to stay in a better hotel. For years the players had felt comfortable in these sur-roundings, and they would not stay anywhere else. This is also a form of superstition. The same holds true that you have to quit staying at a first class hotel when such a stay is always followed by a bad result. When thinking level-headedly, you have to conclude that there is no relation between the hotel and the performance on the field. However, it is not sensible in light of the psychological team building process to not take this into account; in particular because the coach is also influ-enced by some form of superstition. Anyone who works in an atmos-phere where achievements need to be made is aquatinted with exam-ples of these superstitions. Most of these are considered 'normal'. They range from inseparable pieces of clothing to a fixed order when seeing the physio or when entering the field.

BEFORE TOURNAMENTS

During the preparation to an important tournament, for example a European or World Championship, you spend an extended period in a training camp with the team. At these camps there are a number of 'empty' hours that need to be filled by this group, which is exclusively made up of males, who all happen to be millionaires.
This demands that all have the willingness to make the best of the situation, otherwise it is a waste of time and effort. This is how I always approached this situation. You can focus on the negative aspects, which can always be found, but then the hours will seem like days.

You have to arrange sufficient opportunities so the players can recreate during their free hours at a training camp. To prepare for the World Cup of 1990, the national team resided at a former monastery in Yugoslavia. It was a gorgeous structure to photograph, but there were no facilities at all. Furthermore, it rained the whole week when we were there, which explained the gloomy mood in the team. Such a week is of course detrimental to the psychological team building process. The manager in charge of football technical affairs and the coach can do miracles in that area by having the right attitude toward the opportunities, the expectation level of the group and the habits.

Another example: One time with the national team we were staying at a very bad hotel in Kiev. The rooms were too small, not very well kept and with no facilities. Everyone was complaining. At a team meeting I had to deal with this. I told the players how I had to 'battle' with the curtains that were both too short and not wide enough to cover the window. I had to do my best to try and keep the room as dark as possible, so I would not be woken up in the early morning hours. The team had a good laugh about it and from that moment on the peculiar circumstances at the hotel had a positive influence on the mental team building process.

TRADITION

When holding a training camp that lasts a few weeks you have to deal with all kinds of problems. The quality of the hotel and the facilities must be exceptionally good. It is not always easy to find the ideal hotel. Another important aspect is to find a good balance between tension and relaxation. One staff member should be in charge of setting up a good recreational program. Also, the time that can be spent with family is important. The day after a match, the players of the Dutch national team always have a day off that they are allowed to spend with their loved ones. It gives the group an opportunity to break with the daily routine.

In 1988, during the preparations for the European Championships, I decided to break with the regular training pattern and organize a walk through the woods. This stroll would end at a restaurant where we would drink coffee and eat pastries. A large number of football players do not really enjoy going for a walk. However, for the coach such a long walk can produce some new information about the group. You can talk to an individual player and you can observe which players talk to each other. It just gives you different information about players than the info you get in a training session.

The team manager had organized a nice walk. At the start I 'comforted' the players and told them that the walk would last 1 hour maximum. After 55 minutes I realized that we had not reached our destination by far. The first cynical remarks from the players started coming. After exactly 1 hour I stopped and told our team manager: 'Well Karel, we have walked for exactly 1 hour. This is our final destination. Can you arrange a bus?' And Karel had to scramble to find transportation... The players had a blast and the objective of the walk was hereby secured. This is an example of manipulating the circumstances. You are not always successful in doing that. At that moment, your illusions are shattered but you have gained a valuable experience.

ATMOSPHERE

It is hard to measure the atmosphere within a group. In any case, the trainer has to ensure that a clear set of rules for both on and off the field is in place. However, these rules have to leave room for individual freedom. Small fines and a fine pot do work wonders. It is OK for the coach to break a rule once to show he is human. Players accept the rules as long as they are strictly enforced on the others, but not on themselves. Where have I heard that before?

The atmosphere depends on the willingness of the group members to make something of it together with the pursuit of success as the central theme. Sometimes factors from outside the team can have a negative influence on the atmosphere within the team no matter how much attention you give this.

An example is the commotion that developed around the wives of the German national team players during World Cup '94 in the USA. The Germans are masters in perfectly organizing a pre tournament period. They have a lot of experience in ensuring this perfection. All seemed to be in perfect order in America. Who would expect that a few wives of players would create problems? They complained to the German tabloid press that they felt that the players' wives were not getting enough attention. A controversy is born. Some players were of the opinion that the wives had a point, while others believed that the wives were exaggerating. One day everything is fine and the next day coach

Berti Vogts had to deal with a quarrel in his team. The work atmosphere became unfit to win a world championship. This was a reason for
him for the following tournament to hire an extensive staff in charge of
the organization of matters outside the direct football affairs. This
included someone who made sure the players' wives were taken care
of.

SUCCESS

Naturally, success is an ideal binding agent and a way of motivation.
The best proof of this is the Danish team during Euro '92 in Denmark.
They qualified to play in the tournament because the team from
Yugoslavia was suspended from participating due to political reasons.
The Danish team started the tournament without being able to properly
prepare and therefore they were seen as outsiders to win the tournament. In pool play they had only managed to gain 1 point in the first
two matches. With one game to play, they had nothing to lose. With an
unbelievably strong mentality they beat France 2-1, and qualified for the
quarterfinals. After a sensational win in the quarters, they beat the team
from the Netherlands after taking penalty kicks. Then the team of coach
Richard Möller-Nielsen even beat the Germans 2-0 in the championship
match. This was an achievement that nobody before the tournament
would have thought possible. This championship was the direct result
of the team building process that took place after the team unexpectedly
was allowed to participate in the tournament and after beating France.
        When successes follow one after the other, a dangerous situa-
tion might occur: overestimating oneself and an abundance of self-confidence, even if it is an unconscious process. Teams from the
Netherlands have this problem when they are successful. It does not
matter what you do as the coach, the 'between-the-ears-syndrome' is
hard to influence. This problem occurred in the Dutch team during this
exact same tournament. We played an excellent match against
Germany in the quarterfinals, and Denmark, the team we faced in the
semis, would be no problem to beat... The result: elimination from the
tournament after pk's. I would rather have started this match with 10
players or being 1-0 behind, that would have been better for the team
spirit! In 1988, it was our fortune to play the Russians again in the
finals, after we had lost to them in the group matches. Therefore, there
was no danger of players underestimating the Russians.

Summarizing:
*By giving a great number of examples from my experience as a coach, I
tried to highlight the aspects involved in the psychological team building
process and the influence of this on the performance level. Without a*

doubt, every coach can fall back on his experiences.
The issues are similar for all of us, however the circumstances are
never identical. Every coach has to deal with these issues in his own
way. A set of guidelines is available, but the coach and the players
make these come to life. There is a course to learn the guidelines, but
luckily not one to learn how to deal with them. The individual contribu-
tion and creativity are important factors in dealing with guidelines!

THE CORPORATE WORLD

Regularly, top-coaches are asked by corporations to give their view on
the team building process. Earlier on in this book I explained why this
is a logical request: the coach has a direct influence on teamwork, the
team spirit, and therefore the performance level. It is a fact that in athletics, as well as in the corporate world, it is important to convince each
person that in him or her a surplus value is present. To activate this you
need the correct coaching, convincing, and guidance. When everyone
contributes just a little bit more, the output of the company will increase
quite a bit. Besides, it also makes you feel good. The request of the
corporate world towards the coaches is an obvious one. Due to the fact
that this mostly entails the psychological team building process, I would
like to go into this in more detail.

THE DREAM

Similar to the world of sport, in the corporate world a lot of discussions
are being held about team building. Important is the execution in this;
the translation to the daily practices. In the corporate world, this is also
a difficult and time-consuming process.

The point of departure is the point of view of the corporation:
The collective dream. What do we want to achieve as a company?
When this vision is clearly described, the next important step is to convince each employee that he contributes in the quest to achieve this
dream. No matter how large or small the contribution may be, there is a
connection between each role in relation to the collective objective(s).
The recognition of this fact throughout the company can do miracles.
Also, a small contribution is a contribution and has its value! The collective dream becomes a binding agent and I feel that is one of the
most important aspects of the mental team building process.

STRUCTURAL PROCESS

Corporations have still other binding agents. For example, workshops
or - in the social setting - company parties. The disadvantage of these
is that they only work temporarily. This is also true about pep talks by

The winning coach carried by his players (Euro 88)

To experience the ultimate moment as a team (Euro88)

motivational speakers. You can possibly (in the short term) achieve the goal that people have more confidence in themselves, however (long term) it is not successful in achieving the goal of making employees feel that they are an important part of the way the company is run. And that is what it is all about! When you want to achieve this goal, the business managers will have to realize that team building should be a structural process just as it is in the athletic world. Team building entails much more than spending a weekend camping in the woods or canoeing with the group. And in the corporate world, it entails much more than a big party, an incidental workshop, or an evening with a motivational speaker.

COMMUNICATION

It amazes me each time I hear about mistakes that were made at companies due to a lack of communication that had major consequences for the companies. This is especially true for companies that have several branches. Just think of Dutch multi-national Philips. At a given moment the supervision fails and there is a lack of coordination. This is the reason why it is of great importance that every company has someone who guards these communication lines.

I know a person who performs this task at the Dutch justice ministry. She has great social competence, is intelligent, and is able to communicate well with others. I heard that her appointment has had a positive effect on this immense department. The communication lines are clear to everyone again. Everyone feels like they are a vital part of the company again.

People have the tendency to do their own thing when they are anonymous in a large mass. They do not take the collective aim enough into account. When I was the technical director at the KNVB I received a memo from someone at the other side of the hallway. Apparently, at that moment, that was the way people communicated with each other at the headquarters of the Dutch football association. I called that person right away and asked him nicely to from that moment on just to come and talk to me if he needed to communicate with me about something. It is 'deadly' for a company when the communicative culture is one where the memo's, the newsletter, and e-mails are the only way people 'talk' to each other.

To communicate well also means that the managers are capable of having professional dialogues with their staff members. My nickname in the football community is the 'general'. This dates from a period in time when I believed that the players were not ready to engage in a professional dialogue. I did dictate from the top down quite a bit at that time. Later on when the players had ripened a bit, I had countless professional dialogues with them. This makes it possible to estimate to which degree you can delegate certain things. A competent manager dares to do this. You do have to be sure that everyone understands that having a say in a matter does not mean making your decisions for you. This danger may occur when you do not have enough authority.

Next to the professional dialogue, we also have the personal dialogues. I do not want to elaborate on that too much. I did not use that type of communication too often, because it did not fit with my personality. I was not the type of trainer who was one of the guys. That felt a little too chummy. I believe that it is harder to make decisions that are necessary to make in the best interest of the team when you are a comrade of the players. Furthermore, a lot of people have trouble distinguishing the difference between professional and personal dialogues.

I am a proponent of running a tight ship when it comes to my authority over the team. When I started coaching at Ajax, there were still some players who I had played with in Ajax 1. As a player I was known as a joker, always ready to have some fun. I of course wanted to shed this image of myself now that I was the coach. This is why at the beginning I sometimes was harder on the team than was maybe necessary. This is a recognizable dilemma when a person receives a promotion and is appointed in a managerial position. However, if I could do it over again I would, when in similar circumstances, act in the same manner.

DYNAMICS

Many staff members strive for set patterns that are safe and costs less energy. However, in a dynamic business you will have to, just as in the world of football, remain open to innovations. Then, there has to be someone who can convince you of this and take you out of this habitual pattern. Only then are people willing to believe that improvements can be made and the collective aim can be realized. Naturally, such a common goal can not be achieved right away. Just like a football coach, the management must also strive for realistic short-term goals to be able to reach the ultimate goal.

CREDIBILITY

An important condition that has to be met to realize this common 'dream of the company' is the credibility of the manager(s). When the manager has credibility, the employees, just like soccer players, are willing to do something extra for that person, especially when that approach yields success.

Credibility is based on having expertise, the manner in which you transfer your knowledge, and very importantly your reputation. It is the name you have made for yourself. When Johan Cruijff makes a statement, he has a bigger impact than when Hans Westerhof, the current youth coordinator at Ajax, voices his opinion. This has everything to do with the reputation of both coaches and not with their expertise. This is why it is important that coaches with a reputation make meaningful statements and have a tale to tell that has significance.

TEAM SPIRIT

Every single day, soccer coaches must be attentive to factors that may threaten the positive team spirit. This is also true for managers in the business world. When a staff member leaves a department, the hierarchy changes within that group. However, external factors can also play an important role. In this chapter, I have described the negative role that the wives of the German players played during the World Cup in America. The link to the business world is easily made: conflicts that develop that can be blamed on people from outside the company. There are plenty of examples to find in which the team spirit is put under pressure by factors from inside or outside. Just like the soccer coach, the business manager must also constantly stay alert to guard against this, by influencing this process through good communication. This communication with people from the outside costs time and effort. That is maybe where the biggest hurdle lays.

In the world of soccer, the coach has a staff around him that assists in recognizing the signals that form a threat to the team spirit. A good assistant coach is a bridge between the head coach and the players, and gains the trust of the players by fulfilling this role. The masseur and the physiotherapist also know what goes on in the group. The relaxed posture on the massage table evidently entices players to say what is on their mind. This information might be very important for a coach to know. You do however, have to deal with this information very carefully. When it is in the best interest of the team, I find it necessary to hear this information. However, the player must never find out that the person he confided in has relayed the information to the coach.

In a company, the manager also has the need for information from others about what is going on within the company. This same caution is required in dealing with this information.

GUIDELINES

A company also has guidelines that need to be followed so the discipline around the office does not break down. These guidelines need to be clear for everyone and may not be ignored.

A coach is consequently expected to apply the rules. This is no different from a manager in the business world, who must be clear and honest to all, no matter whom it concerns. I am referring to the conflict with Ronald Koeman during the preparations for Euro '88. In addition, being a good example yourself is a prerequisite for coming across as a credible person. You cannot address the behavior of an employee when you as the manager yourself fail in that respect. Credibility is an invaluable asset when managing.

LEADERSHIP

The type of leadership a company or organization has the need for depends on the context in which he has to operate. Winston Churchill was a great leader for England during the Second World War, but after the war he quit. He found himself not to be a political leader, because he hated compromises. He did not want to play that other game.

After I left Ajax, Kovacs was appointed as the coach. This was a smart move by Ajax. After all those years, the club had a need for a different type of coach. This was the reason for the continued success. The star-players were schooled; they knew all the ins and outs. Therefore there was room for a coach who gives his players more lee-way. Problems did occur when a successor for Kovacs had to be appointed. At that time, there was a need for a coach who dared to take on the confrontations with the star-players. Ajax was not success-ful for years in finding this type of coach. A poor level of performance characterized these years.

The same happened at multinational Philips, when it was nec-essary after a period of poor results to appoint a leader such as Timmer who was able to make tough decisions during the downsizing of the company. After this process is completed, the management will need to adopt a different attitude. For most, it is difficult to change their style of leadership when the situation has changed. This is the reason that at such a moment, the complete management staff is replaced, just as it happens to coaches in the world of athletics.

In the world of soccer it can be a handicap that the executive committee does not have enough know-how to decide who would be the best trainer for the club. Members of the board are usually not cho-sen to sit in the executive committee due to their insight in the sport. There are also no headhunters in the sport of soccer who try to find the coach who fits best with the club. The business world does utilize expert professionals, for example those who sit in the board of trustees or the already mentioned headhunters. This is why it is relatively simple to find a person in the business world who has proven leadership quali-ties and fulfills the required demands. The most important demands are: a strong personality, credibility, educated both theoretically and practically, having clear views, be a right fit with the company and be able to withstand stress. Indeed these are the same requirements a top-coach has to satisfy.

GUIDELINES FOR THE PSYCHOLOGICAL TEAM BUILDING PROCESS:

- Harmony
  executive committee - staff members - coach;
  medical staff;
  influence of the media
  columns;
  character of the players.
- Game- and behavioral rules:
  dealing with criticism;
  fulfillment of agreements;
  fines.
- The hierarchy within the group
  pecking order;
  the star player.
- Kingdoms
- Clear objectives;
  realistic with sufficient challenge.
- Creating a common enemy
- Taking the culture of the club into account
- Using or not using a strategy of confrontation
- Credibility of the coach:
  sincerity;
  based on a view;
  clear objectives;
  personal background as player and coach.
- Consult situations with players
- Communication:
  with players
  special attention for foreign players.
- Training camp:
  during the pre-season
  before matches
  before important tournaments;
  taking the tradition into account.
- Atmosphere
- Success:
  success as a binding agent;
  danger: overestimating and too much self-confidence.

CHAPTER 5

THE SOCCER
LEARNING PROCESS

INTRODUCTION

My position is: street soccer is the most natural educational system that can be found. By analyzing street soccer yourself, you will conclude that its strength is that it is played daily in a competitive form, with a preference for the match on all sorts of 'street playing fields', usually in small groups. Rarely in street soccer do you see youth players busy practicing isolated technical or tactical drills. No, it is always the competitive form, where youth players learn from their mistakes, unconscious of the technical, tactical, mental and physical qualities they are developing through the scrimmages being played.

Playing soccer every day ensures this development. It is a process where it is not necessary for adults to be present. You also learn the team tactical principles without effort through playing the game. Your teammate, higher in the street soccer hierarchy, forces you to comply.

In many countries where top soccer is played, there is hardly room for street soccer anymore. Automobiles now drive where games were once played. The playgrounds are used as hangouts for older youth with other interests. Open grass fields are now strewn with dog poop. The conditions for street soccer in many countries are less than ideal.

In African and South American countries, where the conditions for street soccer are favorable, you can immediately notice that youth players have a head start. They go through a more varied technical and tactical development within their own experiences. Therefore, the "feeling" for the game is also better. They find their motivation on the street to play the games over and over again, no matter how simple they are. Even if there is only a wall at their disposal... Above all, they possess an agility, coordination, and basic speed which players in Western Europe do not possess as much anymore. There are good reasons that these countries are so intensively scouted by, for example, top clubs from Western Europe.

ALTERNATIVES FOR STREET SOCCER

I began in 1985, together with other members of the then technical staff of the KNVB, to lay the groundwork for necessary alternatives for the unfortunate decline in the street soccer phenomenon. At that time, street soccer was not recognized as an ideal learning process. That came about as the adults themselves became involved and the youth education system became structured. A development by trial and error, with many mistakes and misconceptions along the way. Still, only the adults were capable of developing the alternatives for the street soccer learning process. That occurred with a lot of good will. In the beginning, there was not much insight into the norms and values of the natural learning process, 'street soccer'.

Since 1985, the Netherlands has taken a pioneering role in the search for these alternatives. The groundwork was laid that year through regular meetings. All the national staff coaches, thus also the coaches of the national youth teams, came to Zeist (the national headquarters for the KNVB or Royal Dutch Football Association) weekly to discuss with each other the future of soccer. From these meetings came forth the urge to improve youth soccer and therefore soccer in its entirety. The street soccer phenomenon was the starting point.

A very important conclusion was formed through the search for alternatives for street soccer regarding the enormous difference in 'training time'. You played street soccer every day, often for many hours at a time, sometimes as many as 25 hours per week. In the place of this came an organized uniform training and a weekly match at the club. What happened at amateur clubs, especially with the youngest youth players was that players received only one or two hours of training per week. Earlier 25 hours per week was the natural learning process on the street. Now only two hours of training per week with a club... A 'mission impossible' so to say.

When I was young, you had to be 12 years old to join a soccer club. However, between 6 and 12 years old, we received the most optimal development possible for a young player by playing on the street. There is no doubt possible. My experience is, in fact, that in the period between the age of 12 and 18, I did not learn much individually while at the club. The organized training, once a week, did not add much. Luckily for us, the soccer we played in the street, the fields, and the beach continued to develop us. We did learn something from playing the 11 v 11 league matches, which were a new experience for us. They were more complex with real match resistances. 'Teamwork' played a greater role.

When street soccer disappeared more and more, this left only one or two hours for young players to train. They trained under the guidance of adults, who came up understandably short in soccer and training knowledge. Our study group searched therefore, from 1985, for alternatives so that the clubs could get the maximum efficiency from the two hours of training. That meant years of research and organizing training camps for the youngest age groups. The combination of theory and practice delivered a number of important insights with regard to youth training for the 6-12 year old age group. A random selection:

▸ In training, the soccer scrimmage form must be used most of the time, just as in street soccer. In this form, it is essential to once again play real soccer. This develops a combination of technical, tactical, physical, and mental qualities. Thus, no more separate training for technical or physical aspects as the 'main course'. The very few training activities at a club may not be allowed to be activities with little or   no solutions to real soccer situations, such as running laps, coordination training, isolated sprint training or individual techniques to get past an opponent, running technique, and endless dribbling drills. It is a shameful waste of valuable time. Furthermore, these training forms do not inspire or motivate, because they do not connect with the real soccer enthusiasts, to what they are looking for in the game of soccer, no matter how young. Players must contin- ually be confronted with exercises in training that contain the ingredients from the real game, so the required match qualities of 4v4, 7v7, and 11v11, can be developed. Of course ball skills (trapping and receiving the ball), passing, dribbling, moves to go around an opponent, shooting and heading are developed. However, they are developed only as a means to solve a problem in the game. Thus, it is a functional development.

▸ A good youth trainer is able to offer his group a number of basic games (5v2, 4v2, 6v3, etc.), related to all kinds of complex soccer game situations. From simple to complex forms with nearly infinite variations. The coach should recognize new coaching moments, and have a knack for using these forms. With that, he must watch out for 'over coaching'. The better the youth trainer coaches, and with that he takes into account the soccer maturity of the group, the better he can bring the basic games to life and work more efficiently! Due to the lack of time, working efficiently is a very important starting point. To recog- nize coaching moments and give the appropriate coaching remarks requires command over the subject matter. Unfortunately, this is a problem for many good intentioned vol- unteers, parents for example, who have no education in the functions of the youth coach. They turn to training activities that keep the children nice and busy, but within the soccer learning process are not very effective. This group of activity leaders would surely be better off if they held a half hour 'scrimmage' game instead of dribbling around cones for the same amount of time.

▶ There is, next to the two hours of training at the club, a need for more time for the technical qualities to develop. Youth players must receive 'homework' as a component of the training that can be tested during the warming-up.

▶ The competitive match 4v4 (6 to 8 years old), 7v7 (8 to 10 years old), 11v11 (11 years and older) must be, just as with the adult players, the source of the subject matter for the next training. The most important technical aspects serve as the starting point for the warming-up and homework.

▶ Coaches specifically educated for youth are a must. Parents and team leaders must, as much as possible, concern themselves with an optimal youth education. It is usually a prerequisite for successful 'homework' and heightens the chance that the young players are allowed to play in an atmosphere that belongs with their age category.

▶ The pure enjoyment is the game's ideal motivation to play often, and to want to become better. The right atmosphere allows children to be open for shaping their character, provided a good framework is in place.

▶ Generally speaking, there are only a few natural (top) talents! Youth trainers therefore work more often with players of limited talent who are able to learn to become good players in a specific position. These players will from here on be called the 'work talent'! The biggest group is the recreational players. From a social standpoint this is the most important group. After their active career as a soccer player they can become referees, linesmen, volunteers, board members, and caretakers. They are indispensable at every club. Clubs must therefore take care to maintain, especially nowadays, a good social climate. The older youth players need to be involved, especially with the athletic aspects of the club. Soccer as a movement sport is important in a world wherein people are more and more passive in regards to physical activity. For all these recreational players, the youngest youth group lays the basis for a unique atmosphere, which will always remain with them, no matter what direction they choose. The same goes for me with my unforgettable memories of street soccer.

In fifteen years time we have made enormous structural progress in youth soccer in the Netherlands. The fast changing social circumstances require however, that we continue to be open to changes and new alternatives.

FOCUS ON THE CHILD

In contrast to soccer for adults, individual development is central in youth soccer. Yet, also with youth players there is already some team tactical development present. A trainer should not impose these team tactics on the youth players. In youth soccer, a good trainer coaches team tactics with the greatest of ease. He must be conscious that it is not the result, but the enjoyment of the game that is essential. The youth coach must convince his players that team tactics are necessary to win the match. And everyone wants to win! Winning is the raisins in the soccer oatmeal.

The urge to win is used by a good youth coach to develop the principles of teamwork without effort. That is why general tactical guidelines are necessary. The youth players pick it up out of their own free will. The result is not allowed to be central, but the quality of play and the enjoyment should be central. In youth soccer, this important basic assumption is often sinned against. Youth trainers and parents want to win at all costs. Consequently, over a period of time the enjoyment of the game disappears and the youth players drop out. The will to win must come from within the child. Parents, activity leaders, and trainers must only create conditions, through organizing matches and giving training sessions, in keeping with the perceived world of the child. His urge to win and the perceived atmosphere make the child ripe for development as a soccer player and a person, with the accent on the first.

Nevertheless, it is important to employ the team building process as young as possible, even with the youngest age group category. Teambuilding is a step-by-step educational mechanism. It occurs in the young age groups with many simple guidelines such as looking for open space, trying to win the ball back as soon as it is lost and making the field as big as possible. Consequently, the young players start to function better within the team framework. Unconsciously, through positively influencing each other, each individual can reach his or her potential. The insight into coming up with the solutions to game situations, and within the coherence of these solutions to make the team play better soccer, will raise the enjoyment of the game. Players learn to play the game in a more fun manner. First in forms such as 4v4 and 7v7, and finally at about 11 years old, in the most difficult form: 11v11.

It is a shame that in many countries youth players are harnessed to tactics by their coaches at too early an age. At this stage, there is too little room for the unconstrained development of abilities. The cause? Too many youth coaches think their own success with the team is very important. This is at the expense of the unconstrained development of the youth players. Physical strength then often goes before soccer skill.

Youth teams from the Netherlands seldom perform well at the international level. They play nice soccer, but with mediocre results. Only later, as the players are adult soccer players, does this development deliver the optimal results. Especially for a more attacking and adventurous playing style, an unconstrained development is essential. In many countries, the development of the young players is inhibited. The players do not reach their full potential because they are too early on sacrificed for the result. Their development is stagnated for the principle 'the result takes precedent over how it is achieved'. They are surely not educated to play very creative, attacking soccer. Luckily, there are countries such as the Netherlands, Portugal, Denmark, Spain, and Brazil, where it works differently. It is a shame that in some of these countries, such as Portugal and Spain, the national teams do not build upon this outstanding youth education. They lapse into yet another much too defensive and fearful playing style. Lately, especially in Spain, there has been a change.

GUIDELINES FOR EACH AGE CATEGORY

In the structure of the total youth soccer learning process, the team building methodology must play an integral part as an extra quality in individual development. It is once more an alternative for the disappearance of 'the street soccer learning process'. From 5 to 17 years old, the team building process first takes place unconsciously, and then as the players become older, becomes increasingly more deliberate. It is a step-by-step development that moves from offering team tactical elements with ease to the imposition of clear cut written tasks and functions within an optimally developed playing style.
I will now delve deeper into the consequences of it for the different age groups.

INDIVIDUALLY PLAYING WITH THE BALL
(5 YEARS OLD)

The first phase is the introductory period, where the child is not ready for doing something with others. The ball is for him or her. This affinity for the ball must set in. The unity of the child and the ball limits the activities. Fantasy- and skill games can be on the menu. Surely not team building. It is all about the youngest players: the youth players from about 5 years old.

7v7 and 11v11 are useless means for their development. The game is too complex; the field is too big. For these beginners a simplified form is better. The most simplified form, wherein the ingredients of the match can be found, is 4v4 with small goals (3x1 meter). There is no talk over specialization and thus no preference for a particular position. At this age with 4v4, there are no goalkeepers, only 'flying keepers' (the closest player to the goal at a particular time becomes the keeper). The specialization as a goalkeeper should not be permitted to begin too early. There is still enough time! Learn soccer! A general technical-tactical development takes preference in this age group. To prevent misunderstandings: by choosing for 4v4, forms such as 5v5 or 6v6 are not being declared as unsuitable. However, they simply demand something more from the quality of the players in the area of positional play. Therefore, the technical department of the KNVB in the Netherlands chose 4v4 as the starting point of the organized, local competition form, most often organized as tournaments.
Shooting and heading are not required basic skills for this age group. There is more strength needed for that!

TO FURTHER DEVELOP THE QUALITIES TO PLAY 4V4 AND 7V7 (6-8 YEARS OLD)

In the age category 6 to 8 years old, known as F-youth in the Netherlands, 11v11 is still a useless means for their development. The game is still too complex; the field is still too big. For these beginners simplified forms of 4 v4 and 7v7 are better suited. The official match organization for these players is 7v7. However, also among the very youngest there are already talented and advanced players. They are ready earlier to play a more complex form. At top clubs such as Ajax, 7 year olds play 11v11 in a sound manner. There is nothing against this: not the calendar-, but the soccer-age (the level of development) and the match aptitude are the determining factors.

Specific points of attention with the youngest players are the basic technical skills involved in playing 4v4 in training and 7v7 in matches: passing, receiving, and dribbling - to advance the ball or to beat an opponent. Game forms are central during the training of the F-players, and serve as the basis wherein ingredients such as time, space, direction, speed, opponents, enjoyment, and challenge play a role. The good cook (coach) knows how to play with these ingredients, by which game situations are constantly being created that are a challenge for the youth players. The secret of the craftsman is therefore to improve the technical skills while at the same time employing as great a variety of soccer activities as possible. The technical skills need to be functionally developed. Technical skills and tactical insight are therefore required to go hand in hand. A golden rule.

From out of the natural urge to want to win the official 7v7 match, the F-youth stand open for the most simple teamwork ingredients. Therefore for team building! Elementary tasks such as staying involved in the play when your team has possession of the ball and when the other team has the ball, covering the complete space of the field, and avoiding ball chasing are involved. These are the elements of soccer, which can be presented to this age group, but are not to be imposed on the players. So the trainer of the F-youth must never stand before the group and say: "We will do it this way today and whoever does not listen, will not play anymore..."

Notice what they can do with simple guidelines. You can, in a playful manner, make it clear to the F-youth that the chance to win is small if you want the ball all to yourself... You surely heard it when playing street soccer when you hogged the ball.

Use the 4v4 match to make it clear in training sessions. This is not simple didactically. You must speak the language of the child and thus put yourself in the shoes of the child. Who can do that? Coaches and team leaders who are specifically educated, but also former players, older youth players, and do not forget ex-trainers from senior teams, who because of their age might have to drop out. Training youth is wonderful work and keeps you young.

The second year F-youth are often able to solve simple match situations with their own soccer experience. They first learn to understand the fundamentals of team tactical elements and then use them in their play. The dribbling technique requires still further development. Alas, the importance of this aspect as an isolated training drill is overestimated. You can easily fill up the training time with this, mostly with endless variations. But remember that the dribbling technique is a means for a functional move. It is a prerequisite to learning how to get past an opponent. It is not about tricks! 1v1 situations with a conclusion such as with a chance to score in the end are ideal dribbling activities. The new ingredients are shooting and dribbling competitions with shooting as well. In addition, do not forget: larger goals are now used and there is now a real goalkeeper. Training activities shall therefore be more varied. However, relatively little training time should be spent on dribbling without resistance. The nucleus of the training for the F-youth must be the game form, one in which the complexity fits with their qualities.

TO FURTHER DEVELOP THE QUALITIES TO PLAY 7V7 (8 TO 10 YEARS OLD)

With the 8-10 year olds, the E-youth, 7v7 is the official competition form and thereby the starting point for the training forms. 7v7 is more complex and places higher demands on individual qualities and teamwork.

The three team functions stand out more from each other. As with 4v4, the simple team tactical aspects are offered, but not imposed. When youth players only see a training form as an assignment from the trainer that they must carry out, the motivation and performance will quickly decrease. Giving meaning to the training is crucial.

The training activities in this age group are not so different from those in the F-youth. The resistances in the different game forms increase. The E-youth must play in a larger area, but have less time to handle the ball. It is becoming more of a job of insight into the game and seeing the field. The number of duels increase.

The coach must go over different game ingredients, because the field is larger and the game situations are becoming more complex. The basic form, wherein the match ingredients are efficiently incorporated, remains vital. The manner in which they experience the training and constant repetition guarantee an optimal learning process.

For the individual technical development, 'homework' remains very important. During the training give the youth players things they can practice in their own neighborhoods, the well-known Coerver-techniques for example. Tell them that the techniques are needed in order to play the game and devote time during the next training to go over it. 'Homework monitoring' stimulates and motivates.

Remarks:

Let me digress. Recently in a woods in Zeist, I saw a mother with two children and a dog step out of a car. The dog at once began to run, intuitively knowing the surroundings as an area for playing. With the children it was, remarkably enough, not the case. Their mother had to come up first with a number of ideas. At that moment, I realized that nowadays children no longer recognize many locations as places to play. In their own perception of the world, a parking lot is only a parking lot and certainly not an ideal soccer field. You play basketball on a basketball court. Who comes up with the idea anymore that if there are four garbage cans, they can be used as goals for a hearty game of soccer? It is the assignment of the youth trainers, parents and teachers to teach the children once again to see the play areas, discover and... make use of them.

The 7v7 team building process does not differ much from that of 4v4. The only areas in the development that differ and are more demanding are the feeling for the larger space and the positional play. That happens without effort: so there are no long tactical lectures. What is important is that through good coaching during the many game forms, things are made clear to the youth players, where and how they are to be done. Use good solutions for game situations by the players as examples.

Youth trainers must be as positive as possible and make the enjoyment of the game and the individual perception of the players the most important issue. Parents and team leaders must also become convinced of the necessity of it. As early as possible, youth players should learn to respect the roles of referees and linesmen. In the real emotional (match) atmosphere that is certainly not easy. Just like the youth players, the referees also make mistakes. For their development as a soccer player and a person, it is necessary that the youth player learn to accept the direction of the referee. A good example from the youth trainer or the parents along the sideline is necessary. On the other hand, the referee must develop a 'feeling' for how, in the spirit of the rules, to call the match mindful of the level of the youth players on the field.

With the E-youth, match forms such as 8v8 and 9v9 can of course also be used. However, they are more complex than 7v7. They again demand more soccer maturity. Therefore, the KNVB has chosen 7v7 for this age group category as the most obvious standard form for competition matches and tournaments. I agree with the choice. Some talented players with the E-youth, the gifted, as regards to match maturity, are suitable for the more complex 11v11. In the youth programs of the top clubs, the E-youth are capable of playing 11v11.

TO DEVELOP THE QUALITIES TO PLAY 11V11
(10 TO 12 YEARS OLD)

The following age group category with its own qualities is 10 to 12 year olds, the D-youth (in The Netherlands). With a good learning process from age 5 on, it can be expected that the average D-youth players' soccer maturity be developed enough to play 11v11.

An important goal of the training activities is to make the D-youth game develop to 11v11. This is a big step, not only individually, but also team tactically. Far greater demands are placed on the youth players.

Game insight and technical skill are also developed in this age group category through the playing of simplified soccer situations, the so-called basic forms. Once more, the game ingredients are manipulated. The D-youth encounter larger spaces and still more resistances as regards to opponents, ball handling speed, duels, and efficient movement (choosing good positions).

A new basic training form comes into the picture: the match with larger goals and goalkeepers, in smaller spaces. For example, 5v5 or 6v6, on an interval basis. In addition, individual training as homework remains essential as a developmental element.

11v11 is the 'real' match on the big field. Preferred positions in defending, building-up, and attacking come to the fore. The individual with his soccer experiences in technique, tactics, and mental and physical areas receives more attention in the team role.

Team tactically, the basic elements from the 4v4 and 7v7 remain the core of the development process. New ingredients present themselves. There is now more attention paid to the organizational form and the task and functional positions therein. The much larger spaces demand better positional play. In the beginning, this will certainly bring about a decline in the individual performances. These players must adjust to the larger spaces and distances, more players, more options that are more complex, new game rules (offside is not used in the F or E youth games) and other allocations of tasks. In addition, do not forget about the greater responsibilities within their tasks and functions.

Still, the individual development is central. Through good coaching, basic team tactical elements become developed further. While playing, you can observe how they handle it.

As was mentioned earlier, the performance level of 11v11 is the starting point for the training activities. It is not about the variety of exercise material. Too much variety in training activities is usually evidence of lacking training expertise or simply laziness. Constant repetition of the basic forms remains important. They must smell like real soccer (such as 5v2 or variations of it). The rectangle, wherein this basic form is played, is a mini mirror image of the real soccer field.

I call 5v2 the archetype of position and combination play. You have the opportunity to manipulate the degree of difficulty in all sorts of ways. You can make the rectangle bigger, play with more or fewer touches of the ball, have a minimum number of passes to score, and so forth. 5v2 and all the derivative forms (5v3, 5v4, etc.) are ideal game forms to practice basic techniques in game situations that rapidly change. We can then speak of the development of functional technical abilities. Only in this way can a player simultaneously develop a quality that is decisive for his level and class: soccer intelligence.

Such basic forms contain the ingredients of the real soccer game. Players do it gladly and it is a big challenge. Due to an optimal experience you can endlessly repeat the basic forms, with any age group.

It is also the task of the youth coach to bring the purpose of the game to life. A youth coach can only work efficiently if time after time he is able to make clear to his students the meaning of the training form in relation to the real game. Only then is the student able to make the translation to the real game. This is the reason for the endless repetition of the basic forms.

Especially in the Netherlands, we make the players at a young age become accustomed to the most important foundation of the Dutch playing style: at every match, thus also with the 4v4 and 7v7 matches, to look to attack as much as possible. That requires ball possession and trying to regain possession of the ball quickly after it is lost, which in turn requires individual and team qualities when pressuring the opponent so they will cough up the ball. The aim of soccer is to create chances, score goals, and play to win. Always search for and take the initiative is the foundation of this principle. This works only if you have a grip on the opponent. A grip on the opponent means an outstandingly organized defense. In ball possession, it is all about creating excellent chances to score through good positional- and combination play.

It should be clear that, from top to bottom, from young to old, this foundation of the playing style can be traced back to the training activities. In the Netherlands we find that the attacking playing style assures the best playing experience and satisfaction. We call this the purpose, the meaning of the game. Just as winning is the purpose, the meaning of the game. Therefore these two purposes must be the basis for the content of the training sessions at all levels. That places high demands on position and combination play, which in addition requires a high quality of individual and team tactical skills. The more the developing player is secondary to the result, the less it is a matter of free development.

The professional soccer world of today, burdened yet more with commercial importance, forces the Netherlands in international soccer also to water the wine. Nevertheless, it is essential that in youth soccer until 16, 17 years old our game philosophy remain in place. No tactical straightjacket. Play to win. Simple guidelines on how to best develop as a team. Everyone searches for his or her own way to do it, with the coach as the guide and not as the commander. There is plenty of time for that from 17 years old and on.

A lot of youth trainers still have the tendency to use different training exercises while training their players. They are afraid that their expertise is in doubt if they do not do it. A good youth trainer, composed in the art of letting his group perform the standard training activities as regards to the game form, however simplified, answers the challenge and the perception the youth soccer player is looking for. Basic forms are a reflection of the 'real' soccer match, whereby the youth players are confronted with opponents, teammates, goals, defined spaces, game rules, and still new options to find the solutions for more complex or simpler soccer situations! The repetition of these basic forms is a golden guideline for every youth training session.

There is also a guideline that every training must end with a scrimmage form, for example 4v4 or 7v7. If the youth trainer has done his job well, the youth player should recognize the knowledge gained of the game situations and make use of this knowledge in the final scrimmage.

THE DEVELOPMENT OF A MORE CONCSIOUS
TEAM BUILDING PROCESS
(12 - 14 YEARS OLD)

The team building process of the C-youth cannot just proceed with the greatest of ease. This age group offers all the aspects of a conscious team building process. With the 12-14 year olds it is especially about the development of insight into and recognizing the consequences of the basic elements of the Dutch playing style in the defense, build-up, and attack. This is true for each player, in his position or function, in the chosen team organization. Youth from this age must become consciously aware that soccer is played more without the ball than with the ball. That means that the more you play with your 'head', the easier it is on your legs! You must learn that you are always involved in the play, either defending, building-up or attacking.

      The Netherlands are known for their high quality positional play. The basis of this style is laid with the C-youth. The first step in team tactics the youngest players should take is to work together while defending to hold up the opposition and together regain possession as quickly as possible. Attention is also paid to the transition, whereby each player, directly or indirectly, plays his part.

      With this the development of the individual always remains central. Also the C-youth search for their own road, and have freedom in their actions. It shall be clear that a methodical development runs through the youth learning process. Therefore, the general tactical guidelines are at one's disposal. So the young players can come to their fullest development due to individual freedom within an 11v11 - structure and typical playing style. It is asked of the youth coach that he makes the significance of these guidelines clear to his youth players. And especially the insight, that through and with others, he makes the most of his specific qualities. Which leads to the greatest satisfaction, enjoyment of the game.

      As long as the individual development has priority, although more and more in conjunction with the other players, it is still the right of every player 'to do what you want with the ball'. The one-touch combination is the most difficult part of the build-up team tactical play. However, as regards to individual development and perception this does not fit in with an unconstrained development. As long as this remains central, every youth player must have the freedom to develop and perform individual actions. His increasing responsibility for the performance of the team will have to give meaning to these actions. At the moment that he enters a professional atmosphere, this freedom disappears. The actions must then become team efficient. A fascinating process.

From a methodical standpoint in the 12-13 year old age group, the accent in general has been placed on the team tactical guidelines while defending. With the 13-14 year olds the guidelines move to the building-up and attack. Still again it is about the individual interpretation of the role of the C-youth within the team functions.

Especially within the group of 12-14 year olds, it becomes ever clearer to the coach which players have developed sufficient insight to gradually ripen into the 11v11 game.

The most important developmental goals for the 12 to 14 age group:
▸ The development of the individual qualities to be able to (learn) play 11v11 as well as possible.
- The further development of individual technique remains central. Therefore, increase the number of training activities. Played in the well known basic game forms:
5v2 and variations thereof;
1v1 and variations thereof;
4v4 (5v5, etc.) without keepers;
4v4 (5v5, etc.) line soccer;
soccer tennis.
- Through the development of the 6v6 game (small field with large goals). Qualities become developed such as:
sharp man marking and clever marking of space;
the transitions (from ball possession to defending and visa versa);
the build-up and finishing on goal.
- Through training matches (8v8, etc.) with functional lines (defensive, midfield, attacking).
- The homework with regard to the technical skills such as passing, trapping, receiving, and dribbling remain important.

▸ The development of the team qualities to play 11v11 as well as possible is furthered through giving meaning to the team tactical guidelines. Training matches of 11v11 (10v10) are the most appropriate.
- With 4v4 (5-6 years old), and 7v7 (6-11 years old), the development of simple team tactical understanding (make use of the playing space together; don't come to the ball at the same time; participate in the play when in possession or when the other team has the ball; the meaning of working as a team) into playing a more

simple team role during defending and attacking (7v7) is done 'with ease'. 7v7 places higher demands on the positional and combination play.

- With 11v11 the development of preferred roles for players within the real match begins. That means development of the insight into the main role while defending, building-up or attacking. It also means insight into the supporting roles. This has to do more with the cohesiveness. The larger dimensions of the field also demand better positional play.

A golden rule: once again the individual action is the most important (and takes the most guts and encouragement to do). Teamwork must result from the interpretation of the simple team tactical guidelines, through the coach and the search for combination play. Let them play. They will find this out for themselves through the interpretation and the coaching.

Remark:

It is a big step from 7v7 to 11v11, but one which the average 11-year-old should be able to make. However, with many top clubs, from both the amateurs as well as the professional, that developmental level is reached sooner. 9- and 10- year old talents are often ready for it, taking the level of their technical, tactical, physical qualities, and insight into account while employing these qualities in the matches.

THE DEVELOPMENT OF THE CORRECT
MATCH MENTALITY
(14 - 16 YEARS OLD)

With the B-youth, the age group category of 14-16 year olds, the most important goal in their development is the correct match mentality, as an individual as well as a team player. These players must more and more show the intention that they want to win. They need to realize, therefore, what they should do and also what they should not do. At this age you have to learn to sacrifice for your teammates, next to your own interpretation of your role in the team.

It is the moment for more deliberate individual and team tactical training. Which specific qualities belong with their tasks and functions against the background of a specific organizational form? What is needed for advanced positional play? Passing and heading technique become important components. Everything becomes quite deliberate, but never really authoritatively imposed.

The B-players are presented the match ingredients through talking and coaching. Within specified boundaries they have the freedom to act from their own insight. But if he is to be a winner, he must be open for team tactical activities. The team is the guarantee for an optimal match performance. His share should be clear to him and he must work on it. He is obliged to do this for his teammates and visa versa. In addition, areas wherein the player shows talent must become further developed. Who is suitable to which position and task?

To conclude, the B-player must learn to perform simple team tactical strategies. Again the personal interpretation of it receives priority! Everything in this age group is done against bigger, stronger, faster, and sharper players. The match resistances also increase. The competitive match becomes more important for the B-player concerning his ability to develop qualities for a certain position within the team. Step by step it becomes clear at which position the basic qualities of the player can be utilized. At 18 years of age, this process must be complete.

The most important developmental goals for the 14-16 year olds:
▶ For the individual development:
- Higher ball handling speed through increasing match resistances;
- Better insight and oversight;
- Increasing task-technical skills;
- Physical qualities:
  speed;
  strength in duels;
  leaping power.
- Match qualities, that are needed to be able to cope with the greater resistances:
  sharpness;
  ability to take a beating;
  guts;
  strength in duels;
  team discipline;
  learn to play at the service of teammates.
▶ Further team building process:
- More and more consistency concerning the basic task within the organization and in relation to the Dutch playing style;
- More insight in connection with defending, building-up and attacking out of the specific and supplementary roles therein;

- Better positional play and a greater urge toward more efficient combination play;
- Becoming conscious of the general team tactical guide-lines.

Remarks:

▶ All the aforementioned training activities with the 12 - 14 year olds qualify for the B-youth. There is more attention to better combination play within the training match forms (8v8, etc.). The coaching of 11v11 becomes sharper.

▶ Whenever the B-youth, for example, have 3 or 4 training sessions per week available, there is room for specific technical 'homework' during the training sessions. Also, for specific conditioning training, for example stamina-, sprint- and coordination training.

▶ Also, concerning the developmental goals for the 14 - 16 year olds, some players are able to take these on a number of years earlier.

THE DEVELOPMENT OF THE COMPETITION MATURITY (16-18 YEAR OLDS)

For players ages 16-18 years old (A-youth) the development of the match maturity is the most important objective. They have to develop a winning mentality or even a draw mentality. It is the result that matters. The team tactical guidelines for all players are now being put in place by the coach. The time when they could perform their task and function the way they thought it should be done is over. The trainer will specify the guidelines per match. The adaptation to opponents occurs more and more when the coach feels it is necessary. When the coach puts you on the bench you will have to learn to deal with that. An A-youth player needs to prove himself in every match and training session. Important specific development aims for the 16-18 year olds to play 11v11 at the highest youth level:

▶ Relating to the individual development:
- The speed of action becomes more important. This is required because of the increasing defensive pressure put on each player. Most players will not succeed at reaching the top (top-amateur level or professional). Furthermore, the responsibility with regards to the significance of performing well puts an added mental pressure on the players;
- To develop the correct timing for making actions, with and without the ball, plays an important role in the

coaching and interpretation of situations (create awareness):

-       At this age it is not easy to muster the self-discipline
        required of a top athlete. The influence of the coach in
        this phase is invaluable.

▶   Relating to the team tactical development:
-       Next to the general team tactical guidelines, the specific
        tactical guidelines become applicable at the A-youth
        level. More and more, each player has to deal with
        certain team tactical assignments that are imposed on
        him for a particular match. In addition, the mental bur-
        den increases. He has to learn to accept the decisions
        made by the coach and follow the team rules, even if
        he does not agree with them. If he cannot do this, he
        will lack the necessary toughness and persistence to
        succeed.

THE STEP TOWARDS ADULT SOCCER
(18-21 YEAR OLDS)

The time has come when the players have to show their top soccer
maturity. At age 19 they enter the world of adult soccer. They have to
possess sufficient match maturity to be able to capture a spot in the
higher levels of soccer. They will succeed at the top-level of professional soccer or at a lower level professional soccer, or they will be wel-
comed in the large group of top-amateur players.

        For most 18 year olds that appears to be too big of a step,
especially team tactically and mentally. To perform under big pressure
becomes the new resistance for them. They lack the experience in
dealing with this pressure. This pressure increases due to the enormous significance of the result of the matches, fans who are for or
against you, your popularity, the media and financial aspects. Also your
teammates put pressure on you through their criticism. There is no
room for making excuses. You will just have to perform.

        In those tough conditions only a few win a starting spot from the
get go. To await one's chances to play and then seize the opportunity
demands mental toughness. Most will have to develop further in the
second team. This is a mediocre developmental environment in
regards to the level of competition and the way the game is being experienced. This team consists of players of all ages, first team players
who are rehabbing after an injury, players who have failed to reach a
level that is good enough for the premier team and are disappointed,

and young and up coming players. The matches are usually played on Monday nights in front of a 'crowd' of 50 spectators, mostly family and friends. Some players have the courage to transfer to a club at a lower level where they will get sufficient playing time in the premier team and gain valuable experience.

It is obvious that many 18-21 year old talents go through a difficult phase. Plenty of talented players never grow beyond that and many drop out. As said earlier, the transition to adult soccer demands a specific mental toughness, which you cannot develop till after you are 18 years of age and playing against good competition.

Especially during the first few months, the talented player tenses up in regard to his specific qualities, due to the fact that he is trying too hard or is scared to take initiatives. Few coaches have the courage and the opportunity to let a young talented player develop slowly. Ajax dared to do that in the past and they benefited greatly.

Those 18-year-olds who do reach the top are the true gifted ones. Examples of these are Kluivert, Seedorf and Davids. Others must hope to gradually work their way into a top-level team. They will only succeed with a club coach who has the guts to give true talented players a shot. This only makes sense in a team that is successful and radiates enough self-confidence to include a talented player.

I have to honestly admit that due to the enormous commercial interests, coaches nowadays receive minimal space and trust. The team has to perform. The coach must impose his will on the orchestra. When things do not run smoothly, the pressure increases on a daily basis. It does no good to have pity for the young players. The premier team is a team that has to perform, not develop young talent!

This is why the professional clubs have recently discussed setting up a league for 19-21 year olds that will replace the current competition for the second teams. There is a great need for coaches who are specialists in dealing with players in this difficult age group and know the right priorities for this important group of players:

Important focal points for 18-21 year olds:
▶   Generally:
-       The transitional phase to top-level soccer needs to be filled with strong competition. During this period this is essential in making a break through to the top. The current league for the second team of professional clubs is totally unfit to achieve this.
-       More than ever, due to the high demands, the step from youth soccer player to adult top-level player is too big to make for most players.
-       Top clubs would rather invest in foreign players to instantly raise the performance level.

- Because of this, it becomes even more difficult for the 18 and over players to conquer a spot on the premier team or even sit the bench! During this period you learn to roll up your sleeves, invest in yourself and believe in yourself. The moment will arrive and it is the art of being ready when that happens that will serve you in the end.
- Often it is more sensible to transfer out and gain valuable playing experience at a lower level club. This also demands plenty of mental power.
- This age group needs a coach who stimulates, gives advice and counsels.

▶ Individually
- Train extra hard at those specific technical qualities that are required at your position.
- When necessary try to play a different position.

▶ Team tactical development
- The modern coach will apply a lot of team tactical training activities. Due to the status of this group they will often function as the 'resistance' of the players of the premier team during the simulation process in training sessions. To do the best you can in that role and understand the need for it will yield success in becoming a top-level player.

Remarks:
▶ It is to the advantage of players of this age group when they are selected for the national youth team under-23. These players gain a unique experience during qualification matches and important championships: tactically, mentally, and physically.
▶ At the present time, young players in the Netherlands seldom grow up in a tough living environment. Life is made very easy for them and they are making tons of money at an early age. You cannot put the blame for that on them, but this puts an extra hurdle in the mental developmental process. Not just for the players, but certainly also for the coaches.
▶ It should be clear that young up and coming players on the verge of breaking into the premier team must possess mental toughness:
- The true match qualities
  With this I mean the courage to take part in the battle

and not be afraid to make mistakes. Be self-assured without overestimating yourself, be smart, be aggressive, but not with blind rage. Have stamina. Never, ever give up. Understand the necessity of playing simple. Play conscious of your task at hand. Be calm and composed. Have good concentration. Be able to quickly anticipate new situations. Be able to manipulate the referee. Have the courage to take risks, and the next time deliberately not doing that. And, always want to be the best you can be, want to be a winner! And last but not least: your responsibility for the team performance must always be the motivation to perform better than can be expected of you.

- The correct training mentality
Always push yourself in training. This entails a feel for pacing yourself and the willingness to put in the extra training hours to work on your specific qualities. Be receptive to team tactical schooling. Take good care of your body and your equipment. Communicate. Get in touch with teammates. Talk often about soccer and make a positive contribution to the atmosphere in training.

- A professional lifestyle
Be self-disciplined. Dare to live, but stay in control. A 'healthy' home life does miracles. Have a feel for the correct recreational activities. Be competent when dealing with the media. Be friendly to the fans. Have respect for your teammates, administrators, directors and staff members. Have no difficulty with living the life of an athlete.

Is it a miracle that many good players drop out?

Obviously a talented player does not have to possess all the above mentioned qualities to be able to succeed at the top. It is all about the correct proportions. It is possible to work hard on developing the desired qualities! This is not an easy task. When you are young and rich you want to paint the town red every now and then. This is possible, as long as you can control yourself and the temptations do not rule your life. These players need support from parents, team managers, coaches and teammates in this difficult period.

Many a young talent drops out prematurely, sometimes due to other interests. This is not surprising when taking all the choices people have nowadays into account. Others drop out because they do not enjoy the atmosphere at the club. A large group does not cut it because they lack the mental toughness, however talented they may be. They also often lack the technical and tactical qualities to satisfy the increased demands of modern day top-level soccer.

An important question to the coaches of these young talents should be: "Are the qualities of the player linked to his character or can they be influenced apart from the character?". My experience as a coach has taught me that within the boundaries of the character there is room for influencing, both positively and negatively. The living and working environment play an important role. Different people can have a positive or negative influence on the player. Within this living and working environment numerous situations occur that are suitable for influencing the personality of the talented player. Family members, teachers, friends, girlfriends, and within the soccer world especially the trainers and team managers can mold or break the character of the young soccer player. Young players often do not realize that the people who surround them worship them, and are not critical of their behavior, especially when their popularity grows. Such players profit more from a positive-critical guidance. It is more informative to a player when a mirror is regularly held in front of him than when he is showered with compliments and when his views are constantly endorsed.

The athletic world creates, in particular, situations that stimulate the mental forming:

▶ One of the causes is the emotionality that is present in many situations in which the soccer player can end up. It also has something to do with the challenge that is naturally present in every match and training form.

▶ Another factor is that the (top) athletic environment demands that you wish to succeed and win no matter what. This also entails dealing with defeat.

▶ Furthermore, that all of a sudden you become an invaluable part of the team, become responsible for your teammates and they for you.

▶ How do you deal mentally with setbacks when, for example, you have a severe injury or experience a down period?

▶ And, how do you deal with trainers who try to get everything out of you?

In any case, you are a part of a work atmosphere that influences you mentally. Many a player does not succeed, failing in this forming and influencing process.

Can a specialist in mental training play an important role for this group and the older players? Yes and no. Not like a clinical psychologist who influences his patients, but more as a 'psychologist' who knows the ins and outs of the specific living and working environment of top-level athletes. The coach, of course, should first of all play this role. However, at the top it would be all right to have a specific mental trainer as a part of the support staff. I use the term support on purpose. In the hierarchy there may only be one leader: the coach!

STRUCTURED TRAINING SESSIONS

Within the soccer learning process, gradual changes occur in the structure of the training sessions. This is due to several causes:

▸ The top-clubs in the Netherlands, professional as well as well as amateur clubs, often choose to increase the number of training sessions for their youth teams. This can vary from 3 to 4 or even more per week. Most of the professional clubs have, thanks to good cooperation with the school system, a lot of training time at their disposal. At the top there is even a structured daily program for the talented youngsters where school time and training time melt into one another in a very efficient manner. Mostly, talented players enroll in this program when they start attending high school (C-youth).

▸ For most players in the age group 6-12 years old, only a limited number of training hours is available. During the training sessions in this period, the basic games and their variations should be stressed. However, it is essential for a good development of the player that he does extra technical training as homework.

▸ As more training time becomes available, the training sessions become more differentiated. However, the required match qualities remain the starting point.

▸ When the number of training hours increases, there is time to perfect technical aspects in great detail. Certainly after the age of 16, when enough training hours are available, training sessions should also focus on developing the tasks and functions of each player and there should also be time for individual training. It is a well-known fact that top players intensively practice one specific technical detail. Just like a circus artist practices his act on a daily basis.

▸ The demands in the areas of speed, strength and skill will only increase in the modern day soccer arena. Due to the increased hours of training there is more room for specific fitness training. Also in this area much has changed, but the specific fitness requirements of top-level soccer should remain the focal point.

Science and soccer can feed off each other to develop this specific training. In the Netherlands, the trainer of Heerenveen, Foppe de Haan, has done some pioneering work in this area by publishing some articles and an outstanding videotape titled 'Conditioning for Soccer'. Interesting also is a book written by Jens Bangsbo, titled 'Fitness Training in Football'.

▶   And, last but not least: as the team tactical demands increase (14-18 year olds) this will hold consequences for the team tactical content of the training sessions.

ORGANIZATION

An optimal soccer learning process of youth players nowadays takes a total of 12 years of structured training and matches. Starting with the 5 year olds (F-youth) and continuing to the 18 year olds (A-youth) and over. Capable youth soccer trainers, who preferably are specialized experts in an age category, should direct this process. Depending on their age, soccer players in the Netherlands are faced with 4v4, 7v7 and 11v11 as the official match organization. Within this process, there should be consideration for the precocious talents who should be able to make the step to a more complex match organization at an earlier age.

To assure such an 'ideal' educational system for players ages 5-18, it is necessary that in every soccer nation there is an umbrella organization with regional offices. They have to take care that a well-structured yearly competition system and tournaments are in place, with as many official league matches as possible. The maturity and the age typical characteristics of the participants should be the guideline for the configuration of the competition.

The competition configuration needs to be characterized by performance pyramids per age category. A local competition set up for ages 5-9, a state competition set up for ages 10-14, and a regional/national set up through 18 years old. Such an organization takes care of state select teams for ages 11-13, regional and national select teams from ages 14 and up. The umbrella organization also formulates the guidelines for good quality training sessions at all clubs levels.

We notice the need for regional soccer training academies has increased in the process of perfecting the youth education process. These academies function as an addition to the standard club training system.

Despite the good name of the youth educational system, the rapidly changing soccer society in the Netherlands forces the clubs to optimize the soccer learning process. There are opportunities to achieve this. However, it demands good cooperation in a complex structure of political, commercial, organizational and soccer technical concerns. In this teamwork a compromise has to be reached between the ever-growing interests of the clubs and the interests of soccer in general, as those are looked after by the Football Association (KNVB) and its regional offices. In this power struggle, money is 'the root of all evil.'

It is very frustrating for the top-clubs that the best-developed talents leave to play abroad. However, it is a must for every club to have a perfected youth education system in place because club soccer in the Netherlands profits from a high average individual level of talents, a perfected team building process and a correct match mentality.

GIFTED AND NON-GIFTED

Often there is confusion about what earlier on I called separating the wheat from the chaff. Especially at the change over to 11vs11-soccer (D-youth), it becomes clear who the talented players are and who the recreational players are.

In the group of talented players, only a few are true natural talents. Even a layman is able to recognize these players as talented. These true natural talents attract attention early on due to their remarkable insight and feel for the ball. These players are the artists, the creative players and leaders in a team. The biggest group of talents, the workhorses, excel through having learned to play the game by working hard. They are the foundation of a team. The artists determine the extra class of the team.

The 'workhorses' have to invest a great deal in themselves to reach the top. They lack certain visible qualities, whether technical-tactical, physical or mental qualities, but not to the level that they are not able to reach the top. They gain the most from an optimally developed youth education system and are usually good team players. They are invaluable for the team, including for the star-players. In particular, these players raise the average level of performance. Due to better quality training sessions, individually as well as team tactically, we can notice in the international soccer world how high the level of these work talents eventually can become.

The true natural talents can be recognized at a fairly young age. This is in contrast to the work talents, who only after their ripening process as a youth player can be recognized as top-level talents. Ajax-Amsterdam and other top-clubs start each season with a new crop of F-youth players (7 year olds). These players have already been selected and scouted intensively. However, very few qualify to play at the top-level after going through 12 years of the best training. The others transfer to other clubs as good useful players with a small deficiency.

One example: Jaap Stam (Manchester United) is generally seen as the best central defender in the world. As a youth player, he was not recognized as becoming a possible top-notch player. Stam did not attract attention, but at one point he did arrive as a work talent and reached the top. Players such as Stam show that in this group of work talents there is ample opportunity for them to break through. This is the assignment of the youth soccer trainers. We can influence this process a great deal and this is the reason why from a very young age, players should be involved in well-structured methodical training sessions. This way the work talents can reach their potential.

Experienced former soccer players could play an important role in the youth education process of players, especially when their experience is structured by soccer theoretical knowledge. It is understandable that they have aspirations to coach at a higher level, but it could be a big enough challenge to play a key role in the youth soccer educational process.

The position of the work talent in the team does make a difference for his chances to make it at the top. This chance is bigger for defenders than for creative players such as midfielders and forwards. However, there are talented goal scorers who compensate for their lack of technical ability with a knack for being at the right place at the right time in front of the goal. Many a striker who could not make it in the Netherlands succeeded at a foreign club. The style of play in that specific country demands less technical ability, which is favorable for his specific qualities. The opposite also occurs.

Every club in the world buys and develops players who eventually do not cut it at the top. There is no better proof to show the difficulty of estimating the deficits of work talents within a certain playing style. This mostly deals with speed of action, insight, skills or match mentality.

In the current 'rat race' to remain in the top league it is fashionable to hire foreign players. The homebred talents are thoroughly known. The market of available foreign talents is infinitely large. However, they usually do not solve the problems at the club. The panicky wishful thinking approach regularly overshadows common sense. This is part of life. As said earlier: nothing is harder than finding the correct balance in a team in regard to defensive, build-up and attacking forces.

In the Netherlands, we sometimes have trouble separating these events. We live in a small country and the pond of talented fish is relatively small compared to the bigger nations. Therefore, the appreciation should be bigger due to the fact that for the past 30 years the Netherlands has been able to remain at the international top of the soccer-food-chain. That is considered normal in the Netherlands. But that is naturally not the case. Besides, these successes have been reached with a risky playing style. Then you can be proud of yourself! We owe this success to a flourishing soccer culture, based on thousands of amateur clubs that are the source of these talented young players. An army of volunteers plays the key role in those clubs.

This success is also due to what has been developed in regard to the soccer learning process from 1985 till now. The coaching education system for youth coaches and the youth soccer educational structure is one of the best in the world. The Dutch can be proud of this. There is no doubt that also in regard to team building as a structural process, the Netherlands has a pioneering role in the world.

CHAPTER 6

THE TRANSLATION TO THE TRAINING PITCH

INTRODUCTION

The theory of the team building process has been extensively described in earlier chapters. They were often supplemented with different examples from my career as a coach. The next step is the translation of these guidelines and starting points to actual training activities. There is one thing I would like to make clear beforehand. Every trainer at every level has practiced some form of team building and is still involved in this. I am not going to start to re-invent the wheel. So, what is it about then? The level of performance has increased enormously in the past 50 years due to the developments in soccer. Teams have become very tough defensively and therefore more and more is demanded from the build up and the attack. This is true for all the top-level soccer categories, also those in youth soccer.

To be able to fulfill these higher demands, not only are better soccer players needed to be developed through a continued soccer educational process from age 5 till age20, there is also a need for a team building process that runs parallel to this process. This includes a psychological branch (see chapter 4) and a team tactical branch (see chapter 3).

I would like to emphasize at the beginning of this chapter that this team building process is never finished. A team will never be totally accomplished. In small details they can always do better. These details can vary per game, thus per opponent. In addition, the indispensable team spirit is always under some kind of pressure. This is a race in top soccer in which you cannot afford to fall behind. One team will make the other team drag along. This book is meant to hand over the necessary aiding instruments in regard to the daily practice on the training pitch.

In this chapter, actual training sessions will be at the center of attention. These training sessions are for many a trainer a tough assignment. A considerable insight in the theory behind these practice sessions will be a good support. First of all, as a coach you need to be able to properly analyze the game: 'read' the match. Or said more simply: you must have seen what went wrong and thus what has to be improved on. This might seem simple, but this is not the case. The emotions surrounding a match and poor insight in the team building process can be impeding factors.

When a match has been 'read' properly, the coach should be able to describe for himself what went wrong. When he has those team tactical problems squared away, he then has to decide which training form possesses the most and best ingredients to attack the observed soccer problems. This is not always an easy assignment.

After all, you have to be able to simulate the specific situation in the match in a way that the players can recognize the problem. You must create a real match situation, which always motivates players. After all, you are working with realistic goals.

An another important factor is that you work as much as possible with the normal dimensions of the field. When you have fewer players in training, change the length of the field. You should not play with the dimensions of the width of the field.

GENERAL EXAMPLE

In the next pages you will find training sessions which are described in great detail, constantly supported by my views on how to train properly. It is an assignment for all trainers at the top of the youth, amateur, and professional level to train and pay attention to details. In this introduction I will limit myself by giving a general example to clarify the framework.

Suppose that the observed problem is that the defense just does not tilt enough to the side of the field where the opponents are building up. You have to simulate this situation to come as close as possible to the reality of a match. This means that you organize a scrimmage between a defensive block and an attacking block. The emphasis will be placed on defending and especially on the positional play from left to right and vise versa.

To start out, you go over the problem of tilting with the group. Preferably making it visual on a board in the locker room or on the pitch. A little further on in this chapter under the caption 'Training activities based on team tactical assignments', you will be able to read more about this. After making the problem visual it will then be dealt with during a scrimmage. 11v11of course comes closest to the real match. However, it is also possible to work on the problem with a smaller number of players as long as the players for defensive positions are present.

In this case you will be concentrating on coaching the team in defense. You also wish for the attackers to simulate the real match situation as closely as possible. Preferably a different coach will busy himself with the attacking team. Both teams should have an opportunity to score. The defenders should be able to play on when they regain possession of the ball. Otherwise they will not be able to build up and attack within the drill and will remain in their defensive mode. This is not a simulation of the real match.

Over the past few years I have observed many demo training sessions in different countries. I am sorry to say that these sessions often lacked a simulation of the match. They did not work on a tactical soccer problem.

On a regular basis, coaches tell me that due to their busy match schedule they do not get around to holding team tactical training sessions. They tell me that during the season, they can only hold sessions to maintain a good physical condition and provide sessions in which players can recuperate. I have been hearing this from trainers that are working in England and Scotland, and lately also from trainers in the Netherlands. This holds some truth when you have to play two matches per week at a high level. In addition, there are periods where you miss some players due to injuries or national team selection. This is all true of course; however, where there's a will there's a way!

First of all, nowadays you can gain a lot of time by using video in making a soccer problem that occurred in a match clear to the players. The possibilities in this area have increased tremendously lately. This makes the translation to the training field a lot easier as long as you are capable of choosing the correct training form.

Also, during the pre-season, you can more elaborately go over some essential team tactical aspects that need improvement. In the beginning it will take time to have the players perform the chosen training activities in a satisfactory manner. By repeating these activities the efficiency will increase and the session should last only 20-30 minutes.

The absence of a few players in training does not have to be an excuse to not train on team tactical problems. You can use an amateur team, the second team or the under-19 youth team. These players are dying to provide the necessary resistance, which is an absolute necessity in being able to simulate the proper match reality.

Somewhere else in this book I have explained that Louis van Gaal, during his tenure at Ajax-Amsterdam, played a pioneering role in this area. The players at Ajax eventually did not accept it when teammates were not totally concentrated during training sessions. As a coach you then know that the players feel that the soccer problems are their problems. This leads to an active participation of the players during the sessions, for example by coaching each other. During preparations for European and World Championships, I demanded that the players of the national team give all they had during the scrimmages in which team tactical aspects were highlighted.

Players are only capable of fully concentrating on a team tactical problem for a short period. Only then can you be successful. It is better to hold a short scrimmage that lasts a maximum of 20 to 25 minutes in which the players give all they have, than to play 45 minutes in which both teams lose their match mentality.

GENERAL CRITERIA

These are the general criteria that have to be met during team tactical training sessions:

▶ A realistic team tactical aspect from an official match is high-lighted during the training session. This can be in regard to a team tactical strategy; defensively, in the build-up or in the attack, that you wish to develop or in regard to an aspect that is not sufficiently mastered in a match. The first aspect is more general, the second more specific. During the youth soccer learning process we deal more with the general team tactical developmental process and at the professional top-level we deal with specific details that need to be addressed. With this you approach the limits of the insight players possess.

▶ A good team tactical training session needs to have a clearly described objective. It must be well defined and understandable for the players. They are the ones who have to reach this objective!

▶ This objective is molded into a training activity that ensures that the team tactical aspect is actually being developed. A tough assignment!

▶ The trainer realizes that the plotted out training activity in detail has to be adjusted when during the performance it becomes clear that the activity does not run well and the objective will not be reached.

▶ Before the training starts, the trainer has in great detail thought about the correct organization of the session. Also, it is a necessity to be able to reach the objective.

ORGANIZATION

Guidelines can also be formulated in regard to the organization of a team tactical training session:

- Do you use the whole field? Or just a part of it? When choosing to do the latter, you are dealing with making the field shorter. For example, when playing 8v8. This in comparison to for example a general tactical activity that can be performed on any part of the field (5v2, 6v3, etc.). The accent does not lay in the team tactical, but in the individual tactical development.
- How do I line-up my players? What is a realistic starting position at the beginning of a training activity? In addition to the objective, this choice also depends on the team organization and the role of each player. Again: it is about creating the best possible simulation of the real match.
- Choose the exact starting point of the training activity deliberately. This is essential! A lot of coaches do not succeed at achieving this. The start must be as realistic as possible to be able to reach the objective. Assume that the objective is: 'Improving the positioning of the attackers in relation to each other in and around the penalty box or, more precisely, when the ball is crossed and they are under maximum pressure from their opponents.' Where and when do you let the exercise commence? At the moment the outside player - this can be an attacker, midfielder or defender - is free to cross the ball or by dribbling down the line can come up with a different solution. Nevertheless, an opponent pressures him and forces him to act quickly. The starting 'signal' is a pass from the coach in the space in front of the winger. It is better that the winger does not decide the start of the attack. The coach can oversee better that everyone is ready to go. This prevents unnecessary restarts. Thus no unnecessary waste of time!
- It also needs to be clear what the end of the activity is. Players have to know exactly when the training form is finished and the starting positions need to be taken up again. Is it for example only when a goal is scored? Or also when the opponent wins the ball? What are the rules when a ball goes out of bounds?
- How do you organize restoring the organization? Beforehand the players have to know who has to be where, when the exercise resumes and is performed again.
- Think about the 'challenge' in the training activity. There needs to be a challenge for both the attackers and the defenders. There needs to be an incentive in the objective for both teams. And, how will the players be 'rewarded'? They need to be motivated by the activity itself. This motivation usually depends on the objective and the level of the group. For example, when you want to train tight marking in the penalty box, the defenders at the professional level are only rewarded when they are able to hold the attackers to only one goal every 10 times. This

result is probably not realistic at a lower level. A good coach is always searching for the best way to motivate both groups to reach an optimal team performance.

COMMON MISTAKES MADE BY TEAM
TACTICAL TRAINING ACTIVITIES

In the past years I have observed and assessed many training sessions both in the Netherlands and abroad. On the basis of this I have described some common mistakes:

▶ The training activities lack too many realistic match resistances. You can therefore not speak of an optimal simulation of the match.

▶ The objective of the training is not based on analysis of an actual match.

▶ The objective they strive for is not being stressed enough by the coach.

▶ The organization of the training activity is not well enough thought through, resulting in an unnecessary waste of time. This influences the motivation and the result.

▶ Coaches try to train a team tactical aspect in a regular scrimmage. This often does not work because each player is focused on his own tasks when in possession and when the opponent is in possession. The team tactical exercise will only be successful when each player is forced through the organization of the exercise to focus on that one tactical aspect you want to improve on, together with the other players. It has to become a problem of the players. The positional and combination play and the individual activities with the ball, in combination with the different team tactical exercises, due to the large number of repetitions, become applicable in the matches. The team tactical coaching becomes an added individual quality. To develop together is an invaluable binding agent for the team. Players must learn to recognize that this is an important aspect in increasing the performance level for the match of tomorrow. A team tactical exercise must always flow into a scrimmage in the training session. Due to the complexity and the unpredictability in a match, the practiced aspect will be just a little different when performing it in a real match. However, these practiced automatic responses will be guidelines for the team. The individual class of each player will determine the team efficiency of his actions. These guidelines teach the players to act as tactically cohesive as possible. This is a long and difficult journey for both the players and the coaches. However, it is a journey that gets the most out of each player while serving the best interests of the team. This is a great challenge for both the players and the coach to achieve.

▸ There are not sufficient challenges built into the training sessions that can be a motivation and give meaning.

▸ The starting and ending moments are not clearly marked. An explanation is often that the activity has not been made visual to the players.

▸ Coaches want to show off their expertise by constantly varying the training exercises when in fact it is important to repeat the basic exercises over and over again to achieve a good learning result.

▸ Coaches enjoy being guilty of 'over-coaching'. Do not constantly interrupt the play, but let an exercise be done 5 to 10 times. Then call the players together, repeat the objective of the session and briefly announce what went well and what needs to be improved on. Then ask how the players have experienced the exercise. Eventually it works best when the players correct themselves and each other. Then it becomes a binding agent in striving for a team tactical unit.

In general, I would like to mention that even the best team tactical training session will not guarantee success. The improvement of the performance level has to be seen in its correct context. You will always be dependent on the quality of your players and of the opponents. A structural approach does not guarantee that in defensive respects players will not make individual mistakes anymore or that every chance you create turns out be a goal. A healthy dose of being able to put things in the right perspective is also important. To work in a professional manner to improve the performance level only guarantees that you will be able to get the most out of a group.

Such an approach gives confidence, is a binding agent and stimulates the team tactical qualities. With this you create optimal conditions to ensure that the team can function better. However, it is not a guarantee to win the championship!

TRAINING ACTIVITIES THAT FOCUS ON TEAM TACTICAL ASSIGNMENTS

A number of phases precede the actual simulation and scrimmage with the objective to make the problem as visually clear as possible or to let it be performed more technically/tactically.

1. You can start with using video images, explain the situation with the use of a flap-over board or with the use of objects on the training pitch. Some trainers are of the opinion that these

guidelines are sufficient. This is possibly true for players with a lot of insight into the game, but this is not the case for most players.

2.   A next step could be to perform the team tactical exercise in slow motion from the different positions on the field. This is even a better visual aid.

3.   Another step could be that the team has to react to the coach, who quickly changes positions (with the ball held under his arm). During his time at AC Milan, coach Sachi spent many training hours on this type of schematic training. The whole team constantly had to take up a defensive or a build-up/attacking position in relation to the coach/player with the ball. This is definitely not a bad way of training. However, the players do not enjoy doing it. There is hardly any motivation, because there is no challenge in it, and it is not a simulation of the realistic match resistances.

4.   An intermediate stage could be to perform the team tactical exercise with pretend resistances. The match situation becomes more match realistic, but it remains schematic.

5.   Next, the players are being confronted with the most realistic training form. Hereby the coach largely directs the start and finish and the challenge of the exercise for both teams. This direction is necessary to define the team tactical exercise for all involved and prevent unnecessary wasting of time.

6.   Finally the scrimmage is done in which the players coach each other. Here they focus on the recognition of the moments that were practiced on.

Hereafter I will describe a few team tactical training activities to clarify my method of working.

TEAM TACTICAL TRAINING EXERCISES
THE DEFENSIVE COHESIVENESS IN THE DEFENSIVE
LINE WHILE UNDER ATTACKING PRESSURE

TRAINING ACTIVITY # 1
Objective:
Constantly covering each other's back in lateral and vertical direction joined with a razor-sharp man-to-man-covering around the 5-meter area (6-yard box).

The training activity:
After phases 1 to 4, as described on the previous page, through which the problem has been made visually clear (schematic performance), a

realistic training form is chosen so the objective in phase 5 can be achieved. With the league matches being the starting point and based on the team structure (4:4:2, 5:3:2, 4:3:3), and an allocation of tasks that are used in the style of play (flat-back-four, sweeper, permanent central defenders, etc).

Remark:

Here it concerns a component of defending under optimal resistances. In the league matches some more resistances are added. For example: defending in cohesiveness when the opponent attacks though the center of the field, moving up quickly when the ball is won, etc.

Conclusion:

Only in an 11v11 match is it possible to create the most realistic circumstances. To train a team tactical component is always artificial, but by adding the correct resistances, it is possible to come close to the real thing. Then it is sufficient to train the specific team tactical aspect and thus realize the objective. First you simplify the aspects of the match you wish to improve, and then you relay it to the 11v11-scrimmage. Finally, the real league match will show if an improvement has occurred.

Let's return to the training activity from this example. By analyzing the match (video), the coach has a good idea about the way the forwards move around, how they work together and which players are involved. It usually concerns the same 'attackers'. This part of taking up positions must be included in the training activity to make the situation as realistic as possible in relation to the defending positions. In this exercise, the focus is on giving cover to each other. Then it is just a matter of repetitions, repetitions, and repetitions. It must become an automatic behavior. The players must have an eye for the actions made by their teammates.

Focal points in the organization:

▸ The cross from the flank. The attacker may decide if he gives it through the air or on the ground, as long as his choice is team efficient.

▸ Team A: 4 defenders and one goalie. Team B: 4 attackers (midfielders may also participate)

▸ Assignment team A: to prevent goal scoring opportunities from being created. End: ball is saved by the goalie, ball is out of bounds, ball is regained, ball is played to the goalie or coach, a goal is scored on a counter goal, etc.

▸ Assignment team B: create a chance to score or score a goal.

▸ The assignment also determines the end of the exercise.

▸ At this point it is important to determine the start of the exercise (the kick-off). This start needs be as realistic as possible. In the match this situation often happens as follows:

- During the build-up the ball is quickly switched from the left side to the right side of the field.
- The moment the right forward receives the ball in a position where he can begin making an action is the cue for the start (kick-off). In this exercise, this occurs about 35 meters from the goal. At this moment the defense can shift to the left. Their focus was on the right side. To gain time and to control the start of the taking up of positions by the defenders, the coach puts the right (left) winger (4:3:3) or right lateral midfielder (4:4:2; 3:5:2) in the correct starting position by giving him a short pass. This is also a signal for the rest of the players that the exercise has started!
- There should be one coach for the defenders and one for the attackers.
- The player on the right wing decides when to cross the ball depending on the developing situation.

Remark:
Each time the start has to be timed well based on the retaking of the positions and the readiness of the players. Otherwise, the exercise becomes disorganized and senseless.

- After the exercise has finished, the players quickly need to resume their starting positions. That is also part of the exercise. Stay alert!
- Repeat the exercise a few times before analyzing and evaluating it together with the players.
- Variation: the second cross will come from the left side.
- Duration of the exercise: for example, 5 crosses from the right and then 5 from the left side, performed in quick tempo so it becomes interval training.
- Counting/rewarding: how many goals were scored in 10 attempts? Or how many shots/attempts on goal were taken? The coach will let the defensive success depend on the progress of the training activity and the level of the group. What can realistically be expected of the players? At the top-level it would be a poor performance from the defenders if they allowed 1 or 2 goals to be scored. This is also true if the attackers did not score, but were able to create too many chances to score.
- The execution of the exercise must be an explosion, thus showing readiness and aggressiveness.

▸ The coach needs to change the structure of the activity when it does not run smoothly.

Remarks:

▸ The team tactical training activity only brings about results when the details are taken care of time after time. The objective is to eventually look at the game, perform and coach in a team tactical manner. It will take plenty of physical and mental energy to reach a perfect performance, but eventually it will happen!

▸ Earlier on in this book I mentioned that even at the top-level, the quality of the crosses technically and tactically (the correct moment) is often very poor. David Beckham of Manchester United shows in every game how it should be done. He is in a class of his own. This skill should be developed during the training sessions of players age 16-18. It is tough enough just getting a flank player in a position to cross the ball at the top-level. Thus it is very frustrating that a large number of crosses fail to reach a teammate. Of course it is difficult to play a well placed cross while being pressured by an opponent and running at a high speed. Extra daily practice is recommended for the specialists in this role.

▸ Which attackers are involved is also determined by the team organization. For example, this could be the two central strikers in combination with a midfielder (4:4:2, 5:3:2), or one striker in combination with an attacking midfielder and an outside forward (4:3:3). It can be any combination of players who have a team tactical connection and need to learn to work together. For example by taking up positions by the near and far post and around the penalty spot.

▸ Naturally, the second string players must also be able to practice. This can be achieved by assigning a second player to each position. The other players from the team can for example play a positional game on the other side of the field. This is part of the total organization of the training session. Training is work. Important work. Furthermore, no players are allowed to 'drop-out'. In a healthy group the players will make sure of this (mental team building!).

TRAINING ACTIVITY # 2
Objective:

To improve the defensive positional play during an attack through the center of the field. Thus, by playing a good positional game the opponents are prevented from creating scoring opportunities - scoring goals.

In this exercise the striker who asks for the ball (to and away from the ball) plays a central role.

The training activity:

The focal point is again the cohesiveness in the positional game of the defensive block. Just because the focus is placed on the defenders does not mean that at the same moment the attackers cannot be trained. This is why the attackers are coached by a different coach. This is all very logical because it creates the most realistic simulation of the real match.

Focal points during the organization:
▶ The defensive organization is focused on the vertical position of the forward (checks back to the ball or goes deep). In this exercise the forward who checks back to the ball is played the ball. In the next stage the forward receives the ball while making a run away from the ball. And finally in exercise 3, the forward can use both options. In this example a step by step approach is being utilized. Naturally a coach can choose just to train the 3rd exercise. It is important that the players start to recognize the tactical cohesiveness, both defensively as well as offensively. Thus, team tactical guidelines are an aid to improve the positional game and combination play.
▶ The focus is thus on the adaptation of the central defenders in relation to the movements of the 2 strikers, who will either make a run towards the ball or go deep behind the defenders.

Remarks:

▶ Although in this training activity the focus is placed on the positional game of the two central defenders in relation to the strikers, the positional game of the two outside defenders in relation to the central defenders also remains important.
▶ Consequently, coaches usually choose to mark the second attacker when he plays a key role by being a target player or a playmaker who starts the attack. If the objective of the opponents is to lure a defender away from the center of the field, thus creating operational space for a different attacker, then a different approach is required. In this case, a lot is asked from the insight, oversight, knowledge of the opponent, and the action of the defenders in combination with each other.
▶ The coach who is in charge of the attackers pays attention mainly to the cohesiveness of the attackers. For example, one will check back to the ball while the other makes a run away from the ball on the outside of the field. When you play with a

'play making' forward as the Italians do, this player will usually check back to the ball in the midfield. When in the team organization an attacking midfielder makes runs forward, the deep forward will check back to the ball. The organization of the exercise thus depends on the organization within the chosen style of play.

▸ Also, pulling the offside trap demands that the defenders work together. Clear guidelines need to be described, because just one little mistake can mean a goal.

Remark:

Many forwards who make runs away from the ball do not oversee the complete situation and are too impatient. The timing of the run is often poor. Furthermore, the player who gives the long pass must realize that to the forward who plays on the edge of being offside, a split second can be the difference between being on or offside. They need to have good contact with each other. Also, forwards often play too close together and are thus easier to defend.

▸ The start:
  - It concerns the moment when the opponents have the time and space to play a long ball to one of the two attackers.
  - The exact moment the ball is received by the attacker is the cue for the start. Again the coach will take care of this moment, to be assured that the beginning of the exercise is clearly marked for both the defenders and the attackers.
▸ The positions of the players at the start:
  - The analyses of video shots of league matches will give an overall view of how such a situation is structured.
  - Attackers: striker #1 (the deep forward) ± 20 meters across the middle line, striker #2 plays closer to the middle line. The other attackers play in a position that correlates with the other two attackers.
  - Defenders: depending on the allocation of the tasks and functions, in relation to the organizational form that you utilize, they will take up their positions.

The situation at the start of the exercise will again be marked by the coach. He will give a short pass to striker #2 who checks back to the ball. The attack will develop. Striker #1 will act in accordance with the movements of striker #2 and will stay away from him.

▶ The end:
Again the end of the exercise will be marked exactly:
- When the ball is regained by the defense and passed to the goalie or the coach.
- When the attackers score a goal.
- When the goalie stops the ball and quickly throws it towards the coach.
- When the ball goes out of bounds.
- When through a quick transition the defenders can build-up; especially when more players are involved, for example 4 defenders and 2 midfielders (6-block) against a strong group of attackers, the end of the exercise holds more options.

Remarks:

▶ Also in this training exercise, the reward is an important motivational tool.
▶ In all of these practical examples, I emphasize the importance of a well-defined framework. This does not mean that every coach cannot decide for himself how to interpret these. He must react to and anticipate what will and not work in the training exercise. Otherwise it is a waste of time and effort. The most important thing is that the players notice an improvement in the performance level, regardless of how tough this type of training really is.

▶ Reorganization phase
- Quickly or slowly return to the starting positions.
- This period can be used in different ways:
  As a recuperation period after a period of explosive performance;
  As a conditioning phase by having lightning fast transitions. This will demand that the players give all they have both physically and mentally (razor-sharp, react together).

Remark:

Over and over it concerns the sense of the exercise for both the player and the trainer.

▶ Number of repetitions: at least 5. However it is not the number of repetitions, but the quality of the exercise that is of importance.

TRAINING ACTIVITY # 3
Objective and training activity:
See training activity #2, but now the deepest striker will be played the ball.

Focal points during the organization:
▶ How does the coach determine the start of the exercise now? In the match, the moment the striker can make his run away from the ball and the moment the pass can be given should be perfectly timed. To be able to simulate this most difficult situation, the coach should stand behind the defenders in possession of a ball. The forward decides when to make his run and the coach plays him the ball. Again, to prevent bad passes and wasted time, make sure that the actions are well timed.
▶ End of the exercise: just as in activity #2.

TRAINING ACTIVITY # 4
Objective and training activity:
Combination of training activity #2 and #3.

Focal points during the organization:
▶ Two coaches are needed to determine the 'start', one by giving a pass to the deepest striker and one to the other striker.
▶ The strikers have during the reorganization phase talked about who will make the action. The defenders do not know which attacker will initiate the action; otherwise they are able to anticipate.

Remark:
In a logical correlation with the aforementioned training activities, more complex aspects can be developed, defensively as well as offensively.

TRAINING ACTIVITY # 5
Objective:
Practicing a specific team tactical aspect: pushing up quickly. With the aim to:
- Move away from the goal;
- Regain possession of the ball.

The training activity:
After an attack of the opponents, at the moment the ball is cleared (headed away, kicked away or punched away by the goalie) the defenders push up quickly towards midfield.

Focal points during the organization (at least 7:6):
▶ Team A: the defense, two central midfielders (who usually have controlling tasks), and the goalie (the exact make-up depends on the team organization!). Team B: the 4 most attacking players of the team, the sweeper and an outside defender.
▶ The signal: the defenders recognize the moment to push-up, sometimes a few meters, sometime further. Usually a central defender or the goalie gives the signal. The command usually given is: 'push-up, push-up'. The signal also means that all the players need to recognize the situation and act accordingly! This demands repeating this situation often.
▶ This action is only sensible when the player closest to the ball puts immediate pressure on the player of the opponents who gained possession of the ball. This is one of the most difficult hurdles to take when it occurs.
▶ This quick pushing-up is immediately followed by a moment of reorganization and taking up new positions.
▶ Also during the reorganization, signals are given in relation to the newly developed situation.
▶ When this action has not been sufficiently mastered, you will notice that during the reorganization phase, players are disoriented and take up positions without looking at the positions of teammates, opponents and available space.

Remark:
The other focal points during the organization and the development of this training activity can be derived from the approach that was described during the other training activities. It is recommended that the coach determines 'the moment when the ball is cleared.'

GENERAL REMARKS:

▶ All team tactical exercises demand a perfected execution, from start to finish. This demands a lot from the team discipline and input from and communication with the players during the execution!
▶ Taking the mental load into account, team tactical training sessions should last only between 20-30 minutes. By repeating the exercise it will go faster and smoother as time goes on.

The ultimate goal has only been achieved when all the players look at the soccer problems as their own problems. Only then can team tactical automated responses be developed. This will lead to being able to coach each other better. This is invaluable to be able to be more flexible in taking up positions and in the combination play. This performance is always different due to the unpredictability and complexity of the game of soccer. I have mentioned this before: it is the players that will have to do the work. These polished team tactical guidelines form an essential aid.

▸ The limitations in regard to the team tactical insight differ for each player. It concerns this question: do you get the most out of each player? This is usually more than you think. The same is true for his technical abilities, linked to his task and function in the team and the efficient application of his skills in his specialized position. A lot can be achieved, but each player has his limitations, especially concerning his insight and physical abilities.

▸ At the end of a team tactical training session, a real soccer scrimmage that will last about 30 minutes should always be on the menu. You will seldom find the clearly marked team tactical practice activities again in the scrimmage. However the team tactical principles should be able to be recognized. Moreover, within the 30 minutes, such a situation (they are never identical, they are always just a little different) will only occur a couple of times. It is about if the defenders (and attackers) are able to perform the team tactical guidelines efficiently together and recognize what has been worked on in the scrimmage. In the league match, the quality of the individual player within the performance of the team is always tested. From here on, the coach will further build the team however he sees fit. My examples just serve as an aid, something to go by.

THE COGWHEELS OF THE TEAM
TACTICAL TRAINING MECHANISM

The examples described thus far mostly dealt with the defensive cohesiveness in the defensive line while being pressured by the attackers. All of them were only parts of the total capacity of the defense. I especially wanted to show with these examples how such a team tactical training mechanism is put together. Before I proceed with the training activities that improve the team tactical qualities of players during the build-up and attacking team functions, it seems useful to me to first list the most important 'cogwheels' of this mechanism.

▶ The players must have a professional attitude and be motivated to get the most out of this kind of training session. Such a collective attitude must grow and be constantly monitored. It is a part of the mental team building process! The trainer needs to make sure that the 'analyzed soccer problem' is clearly and well defined. He is responsible for the coaching of the players within the training activity. It must become the responsibility of all the players to ensure that the quality of the performance is high. This in itself is a strong type of mental team building.

▶ To develop automated responses, it is a must to regularly repeat the training activities. Each player will develop this and create an extra piece of insight. This extra insight gives the player, aside from his technical abilities, a tactical awareness of the cohesiveness and teamwork with his teammates. This all takes place in a competitive environment. Just as is the case with the individual technical qualities, a range of differences in quality in regard to this insight exists. There are technically skilled players who do not have sufficient feel for this. On the other hand, a technically average player with a well-developed insight can go a long way.

▶ At all times, the coach must be able to explain the sense (meaning) of the training activity using situations from the real match as examples.

▶ The higher the level, the more 11v11 scrimmages are appropriate to train more complex team tactical aspects. Mostly, it is better to find a good opponent to hold a scrimmage.

▶ When the players are discussing team tactics, keep each other focussed and depending on their qualities coach each other. In this way, the team tactical training becomes fruitful.

▶ At the moment a decline can be noticed in the willingness of the players to work for each other, the performance level will be negatively influenced. The players will not think collectively anymore and may draw back into themselves.

This type of training activity is only a part of the total training. Without a doubt they are linked to the improvement of the performance level. Still, there is only one absolute indicator for evaluating the match performance: the final result! 'Too bad, we played well, but still lost/tied the match!' is a conclusion that is based on cheap sentiment. There is nothing worse than to have 'played well, but lost the match'. And there is nothing better in the soccer world than to have 'played badly, but still win the match'. This is definitely true in the views of the player and the coach.

Some coaches in the Netherlands are of the opinion that it is more important to play attractively and to take risks while playing attacking soccer than the final result. In my eyes that is having the wrong priorities. Between the ages of 6-40 years old the most important motive to play soccer is to be better than the opponents.

Is the quality of the style of play not important? In my view it is important, but not at the expense of the result. This implies that the execution of every style of play must possess the possibility to adapt to the circumstances.

Hardly any problems occur in national competitions where all the clubs use the same style of play. This is a different story in international competitions. Dutch teams are proponents of spectacular attacking style soccer. The same is true for British teams. However, they are trying more and more to adapt their style of play to that of the European mainland without giving up their own character and opportunism.

Dutch club teams, who play at the international level, including the national team, had to adjust their style of play. Fortunately, this is done as much as possible without losing the characteristic qualities of soccer in the Netherlands, such as:
- defending far away from your own goal;
- creating a man-more-situation in the midfield;
- a well taken care of build-up from the back;
- and the choice to play with three forwards.

At the international top it is hardly possible to play both for the result and a spectacular style of soccer. Only a super-top-team, individually as well as team tactically, can permit itself to barely adapt to the opponent. FC Barcelona and Manchester United are the exceptions to the rule.

Although we had to water down the wine in the Netherlands, in regard to a number of facets of the style of play, the characteristics of this style persist. This entails in principle: choosing to play an attacking style soccer at all levels. This is called the typical Dutch soccer culture. The foundation of this style was laid in the sixties when Ajax-Amsterdam made a break-through at the international level, and by the Dutch national team which successfully utilized it at World Cup '74 in Germany. A coach who is successful both nationally as well as internationally plays a key role in the development of such a style of play and soccer culture. I find it to be a privilege to have been able to play this role with the support of top-notch players, both nationally as well as internationally.

Such a style of play is the foundation of team tactical training. The characteristics - defensively, during the build- up and offensively - demand a lot of training and experience in playing matches. In addition to this, a specific match related team tactical training exists. The style of play remains the starting point, but when taking the nature and the quality of the opponent into consideration, the coach may want to employ a variation and test this first in a training session. Mostly this means that one or more players will have a slightly different task description. The general team tactical training is a long-term process while the specific match related team tactical training is a short-term process.

Finally there are fragmented team tactical training activities. Here it concerns the teamwork between two or more players. For example between an outside forward and a midfielder, between a defender and a midfielder or between a striker and two supporting forwards. The described training activities #1 to #5 are fragmented components.

TEAM TACTICAL TRAINING
Contains the following aspects:
▶   General team tactical training (long-term)
        -Developing and perfecting the style of play.
▶   Specific match related team tactical training (short-term)
        -Variations of the style of play.
▶   Fragmented team tactical training (short-term)
        -Components of the style of play and its variations.

Earlier on in this book, I mentioned that the positional games on parts of the field (4v2, 5v2, 5v3, 6v3, etc) are not directed towards team tactical development. They are individual tactical activities. The players are confronted with realistic match situations in these basic positional games. They develop insight in these match situations. They learn to see as many options as possible with and without the ball. Furthermore, these basic games are appropriate to develop the individual technical skills. It is about doing endless repetitions.

These basic games are ideal to improve the basic physical condition in regard to starting a run and short sprints in all sorts of directions. They are unbreakably linked to anticipating at the correct moment (timing). Speed is great. Speed of action and acting efficiently are deciding factors!

DESTRUCTIVE TEAM TACTICAL ABILITIES AS AN EXAMPLE OF A TACTICAL TRAINING ACTIVITY IN DEFENSE
(CONTINUATION OF TEAM TACTICAL TRAINING
EXERCISES)

Objective:
Improve the total defensive team function. This concerns the defensive 'disruption potential' of a team or the 'destructive team tactical ability'.

In this we can make a distinction between the following:
▶   The so called 'pursuit of the players in possession of the ball'. This applies to a situation when team A has attacked and lost possession of the ball on team B's half of the field. Team B is now searching for ways to build-up, while team A is trying to regain possession by:
-       Pressuring the player in possession of the ball;
-       Pushing up the lines.

Remark:

Often, the ball is played to the goalkeeper. Pressure can be put on him, because he will not be allowed to use his hands.
▶   The so called 'chasing'. This applies to a situation when team B gets time and space to build-up from the back while team A drops back as a tactical unit. From an organized position they disrupt the further build-up of team B by sharp and aggressive defending. The result is:
-       A poor long pass is given;
-       A square pass is given (thus gaining time);
-       Team A regains possession of the ball.

Remarks:

▶   In both examples it is important which defensive strategic (general tactical) guidelines are being used. An important principle in example 2 is where the defensive block is positioned. Thus, where does the applying of pressure start? This can vary due to the opponent and the flow of the match.
▶   To force the opponent to play a square pass costs extra time. This time can be used to organize the defense better. Or even better: it can provide a counter attack situation when this pass is intercepted.
▶   The following principle is important for all destructive team tactical guidelines: the different lines (defenders, midfielders and attackers) must play close together. When there is too much space in between the lines, the opponent has too many chances to 'escape' while building up. This demands that all play as one tactical cohesive unit, depending on their individual tasks and functions in the three lines. The modern day keeper plays an important role in this mechanism. He must also move with the defensive line. Especially when they are pushed up, the keeper is responsible for intercepting the long passes given by the opponents.

TRAINING ACTIVITY #1

The training activity: 'pursuit of the players in possession of the ball'
Team A is the defending team. Team B is the offensive team. Team B
loses possession of the ball on team A's half of the field. Assignment
for team A: while being pressured by team B, being able to give a well
placed long pass to the striker. Assignment for team B: pressuring the
ball to try to win it back and set up a new attack.

Focal points for the organization:
▶ The start: In team A's half. After a virtual long pass to the
striker of team B, who makes a run, the defenders of team A
intercept the ball. Now team B starts pressuring the ball while
team A tries to combine passes and play a long ball to their
striker. Starting point: forcing team A to play an uncontrolled
long ball or a back pass.
▶ The end: for team A: when they are successful in playing a well
placed long ball to the striker, scoring a point. For team B:
regaining possession of the ball and creating a scoring opportunity, scoring a point (also true for when the defensive team
allows a corner kick).
▶ Number of players: preferably 11 v 11, however it can also be
done with fewer players. Team A can for example have 8 players and a goalie while team B only has 8 field players. Team A:
one goalie, 4 defenders, 3 midfielders and one forward. Team
B: 2 or 3 forwards, 3 or 4 midfielders, one defender who partici-
pates in the build up and attack and one defender who marks
the attacker of team A.
▶ At the beginning of the exercise put the players of both teams in
their realistic positions based on the analyses of video.

Remarks:
▶ Important tactical focal points during the execution are:
- The coach needs to demand a proper execution. At the
'end' of the try the original positions are quickly taken
up again. The teams can, for example, be called in
after 5 tries, and discuss the tactical aspects of the
performances. This can also be done when team B has
created a chance to score. Preferably work with two
coaches who each coach their own team.
- In the execution, the taking up of positions of each
player in relation to each other is of great importance in
reaching the objective.
- Especially for this team tactical aspect, it is essential in
modern day soccer that the players continuously take

up new positions in relation to the ever-changing situations on the field. The players who made the 'last action' have to stay involved! This often does not happen. You can observe that the player who has just put pressure on an opponent 'forgets' to take up a new position.

- Eventually, it is the intention that the players start coaching and correcting each other. It has to become their soccer problem. This will be an important binding agent for the mental team building.
- This exercise demands alertness from the 'referee'. Otherwise you undermine the motivation, the challenge.
- When necessary, the organization of the exercise needs to be adjusted.
- Next to the alertness and concentration of the players, another determining factor for the quality of the execution is the 'rest'. Do not operate too hastily, but instead keep oversight of the situation. There should be no unnecessary yelling of instructions. The coaching of a teammate is only then necessary when he is not able to observe something, for example when he is being attacked by an opponent from behind. Especially when observing British teams, you can experience an unbelievable chattering. This only leads to a rushed and too hurried execution, increasing the chances for mistakes. Each player has to learn to recognize the options he has and to anticipate them. The match intelligence can always be improved on!

▶ Small scrimmages in training (4v4, 5v5, etc.) on smaller pitches but with regular goals are extremely suitable to train certain aspects as pressuring, marking closely, quickly changing positions and when in possession getting yourself free, quick combination play and lot's of shooting. This kind of scrimmage, when organized and coached properly, is an excellent basic exercise on the training session menu.

Why?

- Both teams have to defend alertly and smartly. In particular, close man marking will often have to be done. The coach can easily check this. The taking over of positions after the ball has been lost demands a high level of flexibility in man marking - space marking.
- In these basic exercises, there are continuous quick changes in putting pressure on the opponent and building up under this pressure after the ball has been won. What these basic exer-

cises are lacking is 'compensated' for by the importance of this training activity for:

> shooting under pressure;
>
> developing one-touch-soccer (depending of the age of the players);
>
> developing higher speed of action;
>
> developing a feel for the pace;
>
> making individual actions under pressure;
>
> not acting too rushed (changes in pace);
>
> the higher demands placed on team efficient actions;
>
> the physical conditioning (interval training);
>
> the mental training;
>
> training of the goalkeepers!
>
> And, last but not least: players enjoy this type of training and thus stay motivated.

► When choosing to utilize functional groups - in for example 6v6, and both teams have 1 keeper, 3 defenders, 1 midfielder and 1 forward - you are already working more in a team tactical fashion.

Thus, step by step you can expand these basic exercises into training exercises that come close to the realistic match situation. Your players have to understand this development. Here also a lot is asked from the insight of the players. Not just the coach, but especially the players must recognize the important team tactical aspects.

Out of these basic exercises you can build a mechanism for defending (quality and teamwork) and attacking (quality and teamwork). A quick transition is also an important characteristic, as long as it is done in a team efficient manner and not on an individual basis! This demands a lot of team discipline.

A good team must not only have a perfected team organization when defending, building-up and attacking, but also the courage to use the build-up as a means to have, as much as possible, an attacking style of soccer. This is possible at any level.

However, the individual qualities of the players determine the limits of the possible level of performance. This means that when playing against strong opposition you will not be able to dominate the midfield as much and you will have to utilize the counter attack tactic. This is then a tactical variation of the style of play you usually utilize. When playing a real counter attack style of play, you consciously leave the initiative to the opponent, to be able to profit from a mistake in their build-up. You hope to have a lot of offensive operating space on their half of the field. A lot of your players will remain behind the ball. This is called an economical style of play.

▶   These basic exercises are suitable for all age groups, except perhaps the 5 and 6 year olds. However, at each level there is a different objective.

▶   With the expansion of these basic exercises, other important team aspects can be made clear, often linked with the style of play. Such as:

-     When in possession of the ball, the defenders have to learn to see the possibilities to play a well-timed "pass in depth", whether finding a teammate or looking for the operational space. This feeling for and anticipation of the "pass in depth" is a must in modern soccer, in training sessions as well as matches.

-     The defense (the defender) searches for a positional follow-up of such a pass. Thus, they (he) are (is) staying involved!

-     The deep passes must be given as efficiently as possible to stay in possession of the ball and be able to start an attack.

-     Other teammates take care of pressure in the follow-up phase while moving up (usually in the midfield).

-     The ball has to be received in such a manner that it is possible to keep going forward with it. In other words, turning open in the direction of the opponent's goal. Too often you see a player who receives the ball first, then takes it back into the direction from where he received it instead of opening up. This takes away too much of the surprise and pace of the attacking action. This concerns the invaluable individual attacking quality, which can definitely be developed!

-     These training activities, the small-sided games, can also be utilized excellently to perfect the counter attack or the team tactical aspect of 'covering defense'.

THE BUILD-UP TEAM FUNCTION
(CONTINUATION OF TEAM TACTICAL TRAINING
EXERCISES)

The build-up team function is team tactically the most complex aspect. This is especially true during the past few years, because of the large defensive pressure placed on the player, the ball and the space. The more important the role of the build-up in the strategy of the coach in the chosen style of play, the tougher the execution will be. These strategies, the general tactical guidelines, can vary from a minimal build-up to a complex build-up. From 'kick and run' to 'circulation' soccer.

A good coach, who searches for the correct balance in defending, building-up and attacking, has a duty to the fans to come as quickly as possible to an attacking action.

This means, amongst other things, that every player while building-up (this includes the defenders), must develop the quality to recognize the correct moment to play a deep ball. This demands a technical-tactical schooling, functional skills and the courage to take risks. This is a product of an adequate youth soccer education system! Earlier on in this chapter, I mentioned this while going over the small-sided scrimmages.

In modern day soccer it is essential to have a lightning-fast and well performed transition from defending to building-up. Lippi, former coach of the magical Juventus, is an outspoken proponent of this fast 'direct pass in depth'. To be able to develop such a build-up strategy, a lot of team tactical training is necessary.

The better this build-up team function is developed, the more positively we judge the quality of soccer, as long as a well performed build-up leads to an attacking action in which a chance to score is created, or even better a goal is scored. Nowadays, this places high demands on the quality of the players to be able to combine passes because, and I am repeating myself, the defensive disruption mechanism is so well developed in most teams. You do not get a lot of space to operate. This demands a perfected build-up team function to be able to create an efficient attacking action.

In a championship tournament (European or World Cup), in the Champions League, and in the national leagues only a few teams are capable of creating a chance to score from a build-up out of the back. In my opinion, during World Cup '98, I feel that France, Brazil and the Netherlands were the best at doing this. Nowadays, your build-up has to be of a high quality to be able to create a chance to score, both individually and as a team. In the previously mentioned teams, we see that not only midfielders, but also defenders and attackers play a role in the build-up. In the current soccer scene, this is an absolute necessity. Otherwise it is impossible to outplay such a well-organized total-defense that places high pressure on your build-up. You will only succeed in outplaying your opponent with excellent positional and combination play, performed at a high and efficient pace, with a correct feel for timing (tactical) of the passes. To achieve this, you need specialists. They determine the quality of your build-up mechanism.

To have the correct insight, it is necessary to distinguish the different phases in the build-up:

▸ The most complete is the build-up from the back which leads to an attacking phase against a well-organized defense.
▸ When intercepting the ball during the build-up (of the opponents) and then taking advantage of the not-as-well organized

defense, with the aim to play the ball deep and create a chance to score.

▸ When regaining possession on the opponent's half of the field and quickly creating an attacking phase. This division is pretty schematic. Mostly these phases will blend into each other due to the unpredictability and complexity of the game. The least difficult to develop build-up phase is described in number 2. It belongs to counter attack soccer. The Norwegians were pretty smart during the last few championships. Their motto was: 'Let the others have the problems of having possession of the ball all the time. We dig ourselves in on our own half of the field, and when we intercept the ball, we perform a lightning-fast transition and profit from the operational space on the other half of the field. When forced to build-up from the back, we skip the midfield and play a long ball to our tall and strong forwards.' No sooner said than done. And, Norwegian soccer grew from being a developing soccer country that lost with big numbers at the international level to a soccer country that had to be contended with at all levels. However, in time, a new period arrives: often you are not the underdog anymore. The opponents are taking tactical measures and forcing you to develop more of a combination game. Rosenborg proved in the Champions League season of 1999-2000 that they were an excellent and successful example of this adapted style of soccer.

GENERAL CHARACTERISTICS

What are the general characteristic qualities of an adequate build-up?
▸ A quick transition from defending to building-up. A transition that has to be performed with insight into the situation. It must be tactically efficient and lightning-fast, which not only applies to reacting quickly, but also especially to a team tactical adequate reaction of all the players in relation to each other's actions. This sounds easy enough: 'We are going to have a quick transition'. However, from a tactical perspective, one step to the right or left could be sufficient! A matter of insight into the game. When the opponents push up and put pressure on your team, it may be necessary to pass the ball around to find an opening to start the build-up. The keeper can also be used to do this. When the opponents are very strong and are putting a lot of pressure on your build-up, to relieve the pressure, playing a long ball might then be the solution. Then the problem is transferred to the opponent, especially when your team pushes up quickly and puts pressure on the opponent in their half of the field.

When the opponent falls back around the 16 meter box (penalty area), waiting for the right moment to win the ball and start a counter attack, the player in possession of the ball has the tendency to hold on to it. However, it is always better to pass it, and let the ball do the work, even when you have a lot of space. It forces players to stay alert and involved.

▸ Each player, including the defenders, must develop the quality to anticipate positionally on the quick transition when a long ball can be played, thus staying involved in the play, even when not in possession. This demands a lot of individual tactical ability.

▸ The length and the width of the field must be used as optimally as possible. This requires a constant taking up of new positions. To recognize and anticipate the 'next move' is an essential individual quality which will greatly facilitate the build-up. I cannot stress enough the importance of a quick and efficient deep ball. As regards to soccer development, this requires a range of qualities. A smooth build-up in depth is a joy to watch. Players like to check to the ball. When too many players at the same moment check to the ball it becomes easier for the defense. Thus, players constantly need to decide when to move away from the ball and when to check to the ball, depending on the actions made by their teammates, opponent, and the available space. They must constantly stay involved and anticipate whatever possibilities may develop.

▸ A lot of times a team tactical move may be to situate an extra player in the midfield, just in front of the defensive line. This is structurally the case in the 3:4:3-system, where there is a defensive midfielder (midfield libero) who is the playmaker of the team. In the Brazilian team this player is the key-player who starts the build-up. This player allows the outside backs to participate in the build-up and the attack.

Other teams play with a libero in the center of the defensive line. This player can play an important role in the build-up. Only when it is possible tactically, will he get involved. During Euro '96, Sammer stood out as the libero of Germany, because he chose the correct moments to get involved in the build-up and even scored some important goals. It is hard to defend such players. Too many countries are afraid to involve the defenders in the build-up. They do not develop the qualities of defenders needed to build-up. Nevertheless, performing this task is a must in modern day soccer. Taking the high performance level of 'total-defense' into account, it is important to also have a 'total-build-up' and 'total-attack' to be successful. This is in fact the principle of 'total-soccer' as played by Ajax in their most successful years during the early seventies. Endless team tactical training created the foundation for total-soccer. It also, of course, depended on the individual qualities of the players.

▶ The 'playmakers' are worth their weight in gold, although they have had an inferior role lately. This is primarily because they seemed to be vulnerable defensively in the total cohesiveness of the team and also because many play makers were not able to shine under the high pressure of the opponent. Too many times they lost possession of the ball and created dangerous situations. Fortunately, the playmakers are on their way back, and are much better able to cope with the difficult situations. Many teams who try to build-up from the back do this at too high a pace. Automatically, the result is that they often lose possession of the ball. They are too wild. This is an indication that your player(s) lack the feeling for the situation. Sometimes you have to play directly, and sometimes you have to be patient and wait. This is why a key player is so important. He is capable of giving his teammates time to take up a position. This is done with a developed tactical cohesiveness. When the pace of the build-up is too high, the quality of the passes is influenced negatively and there is not enough time for taking up efficient positions on the field. It is impossible to constantly combine passes in a high tempo. Sometimes you are successful in outplaying a defense by quick one-touch passes. This is a marvelous thing to watch.

It also happens that the build-up is done in a pace that is too slow. Too many players hold on to the ball too long. Especially because of well-developed defending, it is a must to play the ball quickly. When you hold on to the ball too long, a teammate who was open is already covered again. This problem occurs often. It demands being able to anticipate the situation that will develop because of a running action of a teammate or teammates. The player in possession of the ball has no time to observe the situation, he has to sense what is going on. High-quality positional play without the ball, in connection with efficiently playing the ball, is team tactically the most difficult part of the game. The foundation for this has to be laid during the youth soccer years. The combined quality of the individual players of a team determines the limits of the attainable. When watching teams who have mastered this, which is only possible some of the time, it seems like everything goes well without a real effort. First-rate football seems to be a simple feat in the eyes of the spectator!

▶ A golden guideline is and will remain: tactically look to play a ball forward as soon as possible to a teammate who has space or is making a run into space. It is all about playing the ball at the right time in the right direction. This means: the moment that one of the players in the build-up is in a position or will move into a position that gives him the opportunity to play a pass forward which can be the start of an attack. Preferably this pass is given by the playmaker, but this is tactically not always possible. This moment is also the time that teammates utilize to get in the most desirable position. This sounds very simple, but team tactically this means practice, practice and more practice. Also, as the coach you remain dependent on the quality of your player pool.

▶ In the modern day 4:4:2 system, the two forwards play a crucial role in regard to the long ball. They must play well positionally, especially in relation to each other. One will check to the ball while the other checks away. Many top teams have a playmaking forward. This is a difficult role to play, because this type of player has to operate in tight spaces. Therefore he has to be strong on the ball and possess a high speed of action. The attacking playmaker possesses good moves to get past an opponent and has great passing skills. He must be a quality player.

▶ It must be apparent that the functional building-up skills must be worked on over and over again. This functional acting should preferably begin at age 5 in very simple basic games. Without insight, good skills will lose their efficiency.

▶ It is obvious that in the playmaking style of play, the build-up team function is more difficult to perform in comparison to the counter attack style of play.

▶ There are many variations possible in the make-up of the mid field line. This is partly due to the team organization and the available players and their qualities. For the composition of the midfield, it is important to find the right balance of players with qualities for the build-up who also possess qualities for defending and attacking.

With which task and team function is this balance connected?

- With the playmaker, the passer, the key-player in the build-up, the famous #10 player. This role requires as much specific individual and team tactical qualities as possible. The need for team tactical qualities is obvious, taking the degree of difficulty of the positional game and combination play into account. This is especially due to the tremendous defensive pressure put on the players and the ball. Individually, every player must possess sufficient skills concerning receiving and passing the ball, preferably with moves to get around the direct opponent. As said many times before: the match

The coach and his staff: of the same mind (Euro 92)

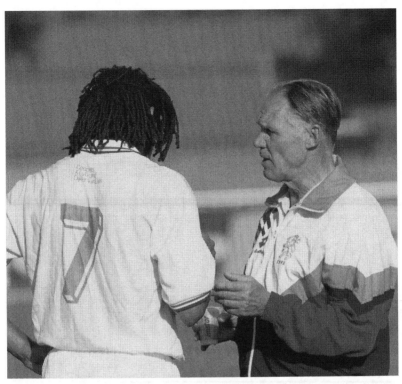

Communication is essential (1992)

performance level is the test for the performance level of your team.

The #10 player is the man with a feel for the pace in the build-up: sometimes lightning fast with one-touch passes, and sometimes slower to gain time for his teammates to take up an efficient position on the field. This requires fine-tuning.

- A midfield with such a modern playmaker possesses a 'golden nugget'. Without such a player it is possible for a team to be successful, but the combination plays need to be perfected and it demands some creativity from one or more players. Many teams play with a playmaking second forward who performs this role in the attacking phase. This is often true for teams that play in a 4:4:2-formation with 'open' midfielders. Too often the space between the midfield and the forwards gets to be too big. This space will therefore be used by an attacking playmaker (such as Zola at Chelsea, Bergkamp at Arsenal and Zidane at Juventus).

Naturally, many teams have tried to play with two forwards and a second attacking playmaker. Defensively this can cause some problems. The team can become off-balanced or the attacking spaces may not be utilized well enough.

- It is important that each team has an attacking, scoring midfielder. He times his runs into the penalty box well without the ball. He is a player who should score about half the total goals scored by the striker. This midfielder also needs to possess certain qualities: speed, of course, and a feel for making his runs at the correct moment. This type of player is also worth his weight in gold. It is one thing to play attractive soccer, but quite another to play winning soccer. To do this you need players who can score goals. You cannot have it all in the midfield; for example an attacking playmaker who can also be the attacking midfielder. Seldom have I seen a player who mastered a dual specialty. Platini was the exception to the rule.

- The open midfielders in the 4:4:2-organization also need to have certain qualities. Over a 90-minute period they have to run many miles. Running speed, speed of action, and soccer skills are needed for the 'train tracks' on which they play. There is a danger that in the quest to get the ball, they come too much to the middle of the field. Defensively, they have an important job to do.

They must have the insight to pinch inside to cover the operational spaces in the center of the field. In 5:3:2 (3:5:2), we are dealing with the same type of wing players, but they must be able to cover even more ground. Usually they have a more defensive task than most wing midfielders. In the 3:4:3, you are dealing with true wing forwards who play farther up than the open midfielders. They have to stay on the outsides of the field. These are true flank players who have great speed, great moves and good skills (passing and dribbling). To be truly efficient, they have to be able to give a great final tactical pass. Not an easy assignment. It is hard to find these kinds of specialized players. They must be selected and trained at a very young age. The Netherlands is one of a few countries that actually develop this kind of player in the 4:3:3-system. The vulnerability of this choice is that it is hard to find all-round wing attackers at the top level who are capable of playing team efficiently while pressured by two defenders. But, as long as they are efficient in their actions and decision making, you can put up with the negative defensive aspects of a three-man offensive line.

- Also important is the ability to defend as the secondary defensive line in front of the backs in connection with the back line and the attackers! The most easily to survey is the vacuum cleaner (Hoover) type, who covers the holes left unmarked by the attacking mifielder(s). Thus, a specialist who has a lot of insight in taking up positions. He is the type of player who stays behind the ball and wins the duels. When he has good passing skills, you are considered a lucky coach. It is important that there is as little operational space for the opponents as possible between the defense line and the midfield line. This means constantly taking up new positions in relation to the position of the opponents, the ball and your teammates. Usually this involves a 6-man-block. Because such a block is constantly moving, and in a well oiled team is inter-changing positions with the 4-man-block up front, this defense is hardly observable.

When possession is lost while building-up, then of course there are fewer players involved. This is the reason for the vulnerability to a counter attack when the ball is unnecessarily lost during the build-up on your own half of the field. When the match tactics are to attack - when down in the count, when favored to win or when it is the chosen style of play - then it could be very possible that only 3 to 4 players remain behind the ball as the 'cover-defense'.

In the Brazilian implementation of the 4:4:2 system, a central defensive midfielder plays the 'Hoover-role' and is able to give good long passes. In the Italian implementation of the 4:4:2-system, there are two central midfielders who operate behind the ball. One of them is a master at giving passes. In the 3:5:2 (5:3:2) we also see a 'Hoover-type' player.

-   When there are insufficient ball-winners and duel-winners present in the midfield line, it will be hard to get a grip on the opponent. This is the reason for the following axiom: 'to be able to develop your build-up and attack well, first the defensive team function must be developed.' Only then is it possible to get a grip on your opponent. When you organize your defense well, that does not necessarily mean that you are playing defensively! The midfielders who are actively involved in the build-up and the attack, and are thus playing in front of the ball, must be in good cooperation with the attackers to cover certain operational zones. The greater this mobility, the better this needs to be developed. This also requires team tactical insight into the game!

Again, in modern day football, the defensive tasks of the midfielders as the secondary defensive line need to be in perfect harmony with the midfield in the attack. When possession is lost: take the shortest route during the transition to defending.

Counter-attack teams usually have two defensive midfielders. But teams who try to carry the play also have controlling midfielders who have the insight and the discipline to stay behind the ball when their team is attacking. This is their main task. Just think of the role played by Davids & Cocu in the midfield of the Dutch national team. Only when tactically preferable, one or the other will support the attack. Also in the midfield of many Italian teams, an important role has to be played by controlling midfielders.

SUMMARY OF THE BUILD-UP TEAM FUNCTION

▶ It is a hard-to-perfect aspect of the game.

▶ Few teams at a high level are able to start a build-up from the back, which then leads to an attacking action.

▶ The 'counter attack style of play' and the 'long passing game' reduce the role of the build-up team function.

▶ The counter attack works well for a team in the underdog position. It is often good enough to win a match, but not to win championships.

▶ The 'long passing game' is not used as much anymore at the international level, because it is based too much on chance.

▶ To want to create and make the play is the most attractive style of play for both the players and the spectators. However, the useful aspects of the counter attack and opportunism must be incorporated in this style.

▶ In the composition of the midfield line, the right balance between defensive, build-up and offensive forces must be found.

▶ The build-up, when wanting to make the play, needs to have tactical high-quality positional play and combination play within all of the lines.

▶ A midfield player possesses specific qualities. The most important quality is; knowing what is going on all around him. He must have eyes in the back of his head.

▶ It is just as important to want to and be able to quickly distribute the ball, as it is to slow the play down.

▶ Playing a ball forward has priority over playing a square ball. Thus, each player must, given his talents and development, have the quality to quickly think and play deep, preferably anticipated by teammates to gain time.

▶ To build-up properly and constantly take up new positions, all the players, including the goalkeeper, have to be concentrated and alert. The taking up of positions must be team efficient. Do not run for the sake of running! One yard more or less can do team tactical miracles.

▶ The decisive factor is the cohesiveness between the players behind the ball and in front of the ball. Especially to facilitate the playing of a ball forward.

▶ Square passes should be given to find the right player to give the long pass. Unnecessary square passes are detrimental for your defensive line.

▶ The better the total positioning of the players on the field, the easier it will be to connect passes without having to look (circulation soccer).

- A healthy dose of opportunism, passing the ball blindly in operational zones is the invaluable surprising element in soccer. Especially offensively, players need to anticipate these passes. Many wing players fail to do this.
- A deep ball to a forward who is checking to the ball should always be followed by an action of his teammates. A long ball should be followed by teammates who push up and join into the attack. It is a common fault that this does not happen sufficiently.
- To play a deep ball demands courage and self-confidence to neutralize the fear of failure.
- Especially during the build-up, mistakes are made. These are inevitable due to the difficulty level of the game. Unnecessary mistakes are mistakes that are being made due to a lack of concentration, alertness and/or not enough courage. These mistakes have to be avoided. A risky long ball sometimes also does not reach its intended target. The player recognized the correct moment to give the pass, but the execution was technically not perfect. This is part of the game, just as a shot that fails to hit the goal.
- It is irritating to the player with the ball when too many players yell for the ball. Only those things happening behind him need to be told to him. Especially in British soccer, players over-coach each other.
- Organizational form 3:5:2
  A quick, well-organized build-up from the back is tough within this concept, because so many players operate in the width of the field (5 players). This is the reason that in this concept the build-up is performed at a slower pace. It takes time for the players to get in better positions to start the build-up. The alternative that is often used is to play a long ball to the strikers. German teams prefer to play counter attack style soccer. But, they are usually not in enough of an underdog-position! The two outside defenders need to be specialists in building-up and attacking. This is why Brazilian outside defenders are in demand in Germany.
- Organizational form 4:4:2
  When observing British central defenders you can often notice that they lack build-up qualities. They have not been brought up in an environment where positional and combination play is important. The famous kick and rush style is disappearing more and more from the British soccer pitches. But fortunately their preference for opportunism and long balls has not. When the Italians are building-up, they often play a long ball to the forwards. However, the forwards are not getting enough support due to the organization in the midfield (2 open and 2 central

midfielders). This is resolved by the use of an attacking play maker. The Brazilians play with a diamond shaped midfield with true specialized players, supported by two lateral defenders who participate in the build-up and the attack and two forwards who are strong on the ball.

▸ Organizational form 4:3:3
In the Netherlands, we are known to have a well-developed build-up team function, based on an ideal positioning of players in both the width and the length of the field. Furthermore, in a tactical sense, an additional central player from the 4-man defensive line is used in the build-up. This player usually gets the most space to operate.

Remarks:

▸ It is important that every coach balances his midfield line on the basis of the available players, his style of play obviously, and the team organization that is linked to the style of play. This is not an easy task. Team tactically a lot of work has to be done in training to achieve this. Repeating team tactical "well thought through" training exercises over and over again is a must! In a well-structured youth soccer education system, the foundation is laid for high-quality positional and combination play. Technical abilities and tactical application form the primal qualities.
With the foundation of structurally developed primal qualities, the coach and his staff are able to work structurally on the team tactical aspects of the build-up and also, of course, on the defensive and offensive team functions. These three team functions are inseparably linked.

▸ Individual actions with the ball, whereby the opponent is out played and a team efficient progression is achieved, are the most fantastic moments of the game. When analyzing matches it is always remarkable how few of these actions are made in a 90 minute period. As a soccer enthusiast I say: what a shame! The reason for this is that one or more opponents always chase the player with the ball. This is why collective solutions are increasingly playing a bigger role.

Let's translate all of this into training activities to aid the build-up. Every coach is capable of developing these activities, as long as he complies with a few conditions. And that is where it often goes wrong. Even at the top! In these training activities, the build-up should be the central theme. This cannot be achieved in, for example, scrimmages in training where it is difficult for players to concentrate on one specific part of the game. The enjoyment of the game is stronger than the learning process at that moment!

TRAINING ACTIVITY # 1
Objective of team A (8 or more [players)
▶ From a build-up, come to an attacking action (a cross, shot, individual action, give-n-go, corner): reward: 1 point.
▶ Score a goal; reward: two points.

Objective of team B (8 or more players)
Winning the ball and then counter attacking; reward: creating a chance to score or scoring: 1 point.

There is a difference in the reward between team A and B, because it is easier to play on the counter and create scoring opportunities.

The training activity:
Team A must play the ball in the opponent's half and try to create a chance to score or score. The defensive block of team B is positioned around the midfield line in their own half of the field. When winning the ball team B tries to play on the counter.

Focal points in the organization:
▶ At least 8v8 to ensure a balanced organization in the build-up.
▶ Team A builds-up.
▶ At least 2 defenders, 4 midfielders, one striker and a keeper.
▶ 3:3:2 is also an option.
▶ Functionally expand to 11v11. This of course comes closest to the realistic match conditions. This choice depends on, among other things, the team tactical level of the players and the available number of players.
▶ The start: the build-up starts with the keeper of team A who throws the ball to a teammate.
▶ End:
    - Team A succeeds when they make the one or two points (objective is reached).
    - The referee decides what can be considered an attacking action and blows his whistle. Also when the ball goes out of bounds;
    - Team B wins the ball and tries to score by playing a counter attack.
    - When team B loses possession the exercise ends and starts again from team A's goalie.
▶ Duration: Play this exercise for about 30 minutes depending on how it goes. After this, a 30-minute scrimmage is played as a test.

Remarks:

In regards to a goal for team B to score on there are two different options:

▶ A 'line goal' of about 20 meters wide. The keeper defends the whole line, but is not allowed to use his hands. Why a line-goal? To be able to consciously keep working on developing the positional play in the width of the field, thus learning to capitalize on the counter attack. Team B scores by dribbling the ball over the line.

▶ A regular size goal with a keeper.
The exercise should start every time with the keeper of team A. That moment is also a time-out where there is time for coaching. Especially by the players!

TRAINING ACTIVITY # 2

The counter attack is the central team tactical problem of the training session.

Objective for team A: outplaying the opponent with a counter attack and scoring.

Objective for team B: intercept the counter attack, then play a quick long ball, or for example play it back to the goalie.

The training activity:

The counter attack is the main course of this training session menu. Team A intercepts the ball during the build-up of team B followed by a quick counter attack of team A. This counter attack build-up is at the center of attention. Thus a starting moment is created for the counter attack at the moment team B loses possession in the midfield, not during a build-up from the back situation.

Let for example, the most realistic exercise start at the moment the defending team, due to a mistake of the team building-up, intercepts the ball. Naturally, every player knows what to do when this happens because of a visual explanation given. Next, the counter attack develops under full resistance of team B. Especially in the beginning, you repeat the starting moment. Of course this requires motivation from all the players, especially at the top level. Now it is all about working consciously on improving the performance level of the team. As mentioned before, this can only succeed when practicing the most realistic training exercise for a short period of time (30 minutes or so). The players should know beforehand the duration of the exercise.

Focal points in the organization:
▶ Number of players: 11v11 or fewer (7 till 10 field players per team). With less than 10 players there is more space, so it is less complex. However, they should be functional groups with a tactical cohesiveness. For example: midfielders and defenders (7/8) against the attackers and 'additional' players. The counter attack is important now,so there should be a tactical cohesiveness in the counter attacking team. The other team tries to give as much resistance as possible. Eventually you get to a situation where you play a full scrimmage 11v11.
▶ Location on the field:
   - The counter attack build-up of team A starts when the ball is intercepted during the build-up of team B in an area of about 40 meters around the middle line (20 meters on each side). Use video recordings of matches as examples for the correct measurements!
▶ The exercise is done on a full field. When there are less than 22 players, make the field a little shorter.
▶ The start:
   - The moment a bad square pass is given (team B) in a vulnarable zone in the build-up.
   - Or for example, due to team A anticipating a long ball played by team B.
     When in possession of the ball: quick transition to play a counter attack;
   - Players of both teams take up a position that correlates with the moment the bad pass is given.

Remark:

This exercise starts with a fabricated beginning. This is necessary to be able to create the counter attack as quickly as possible.

▶ Ending:
   - Counter attacking team A scores, 100% success (3 points);
   - Counter attacking team creates a chance to score, but does not score (2 points);
   - Counter attack team gets a corner kick or a free kick (1 point);
   - Without creating a chance to score the ball goes out of bounds. End of the try. (opponent gets 1 point);
   - Keeper intercepts the ball. End of the try.
   - Defending team regains possession of the ball and plays it to the goalie (2 points) or is able to quickly give

a long ball that is received by a teammate who has a chance to continue the attack. (3 points).
▸ Duration:
About 30 minutes (the first time it will take longer due to explaining the drill and performing the roles as realistically as possible).

Important: next, play a 30-minute scrimmage in which team A plays on the counter and team B must build-up and make the play. Have both teams mastered the principles (guidelines)? Repetitions and more repetitions will do the rest. A lot is gained team tactically when the players coach each other on the field. Players must take the initiative to coach each other.

In this scrimmage, counter attack situations can also occur for team B. For example, when team A loses possession while counter attacking. However, the main focus is on the regular build-up of team B and the counter attack of team A. How many chances to score are created by team A in 6 - 10 tries?

Remarks:
▸ When the counter attack has the preference as the style of play, a lot of team tactical training must be done to perfect it. A style of play after all has defensive, build-up and offensive guidelines. When the counter attack is used as a tactical variation of a more attacking style of play, then it will only be trained on just before the next upcoming match because the trainer believes that the counter attack weapon could be useful, taking the specific resistances of the next match into account (for example playing a stronger opponent or playing the 2nd match in a series after winning the first.
▸ All that has been practiced should end in playing a scrimmage. The practiced situation will almost never be copied 100% in the scrimmage. Every match, including scrimmages played in training, are always just a little different. But, a situation where the counter attack can be played will always occur. The known guidelines remain applicable. The individual qualities, including the developed additional team tactical qualities, will do the rest. This is not a guarantee for scoring a goal, but it does get the optimal performance out of each and every player in relation to each other.
▸ People, and thus also coaches from the Netherlands, are in general headstrong. We think we know how to do it and plan our own route to get there. A lot of good things have developed thanks to this attitude. But it also makes it tougher to get all

coaches to agree on using the same style of play. This happens in most soccer nations. Many a coach in the Netherlands puts play making style soccer (read: attacking style soccer), ahead of result oriented football. Praiseworthy, but not always logical soccer-wise!

CLOSING REMARKS

I have developed a few team tactical exercises for the defensive and build-up team functions. Directed towards:

▶ the style of play you wish to perfect (the development of general tactical guidelines for the build-up and the defense);
▶ a tactical variation on this for the upcoming match;
▶ or a team tactical part thereof (fragment), that needs to be perfected.

The defensive team tactical exercises should always be linked with offensive assignments for the opponents. The team that is building-up will always advance into an attack or the opponent will steal the ball and start a build-up and possibly an attack. Too often one assesses his own performance in defense, build-up and attack without taking the perform-ance of the opponent into account. Again: you perform as well as the opponent and the specific match circumstances allow you to. This is of course also true in the opposite sense. This match phenomenon is often hard to estimate. In a match many unpredictable, unexpected, and surprising events happen. This is why it is the players on the field who should make the decisions. They should be supported, however, by a set of team efficient guidelines.

My exercise material in this chapter should serve as examples. In fact, every coach should interpret this according to his own beliefs and views. Each team is just a little different! What is important is that play-ers are being confronted with team tactical guidelines. Learning to see the cohesiveness of players' actions is the biggest step to take. Coaching each other is another step that has to be made. This is a long and difficult road to take. It is however, a necessary road to take in modern day soccer. Repetitions and more repetitions will lay the foun-dation for this.
There is no perfection in competitive soccer. However, when a team comes close to perfection, it seems like everything is happening without effort and is so smooth that you could just join in and take part.
What is successful today may not be guaranteed to work the next match, due to the complexity and the unpredictable elements of a match. However, structural team building makes sure that: the players

have confidence in each other, there is calmness in the game actions, the essential team spirit is present and team tactical views are present! These are basic prerequisites for an optimal performance level.

CHAPTER 7

THE FUTURE

Dutch soccer has been at the top of the international soccer scene for over 30 years. This is an unbelievable feat for such a small country. Earlier on in this book I stated that this success is partly due to all that has been done and developed in regard to the soccer learning process.

Lately the Dutch teams have not done very well internationally. This is due to a number of general and specific causes.

GENERAL CAUSES

Naturally, Dutch players also have to deal with the greater demands placed on them in the modern day game. First of all, this is due to the unbelievably tough difficulty level of top-soccer. In the past 10 years a tremendous development in defending has taken place, which has become a 'destructive mechanism' with regard to the build-up and the attack of the opponents. This development has been so immense that most teams do not possess enough quality to build up and come to an attack under the high pressure of the defenders. In earlier chapters, I mentioned that the team functions demand to be developed more.

Also, building up and attacking in the Netherlands is a tough assignment for both players and coaches and they also have to deal with an increasing pressure caused by the large commercial interests. The consequences when they lose are not limited to an unsatisfactory standing in the league table.

SPECIFIC CAUSES

Developments in international soccer, which have happened mostly off the field, have had drastic consequences for a country as small as the Netherlands. For example, after the Bosman-decision it became impossible for Dutch clubs to hold on to their best players. Those clubs are also not able to contract the top-level international players anymore. The difference in available funds has become too large in comparison to other European top clubs. This has caused a vicious circle. A team with no or only few top-notch players hardly has a chance to advance in the European Championships for club teams. Thus, an opportunity to receive prize money and TV money diminishes when you do not play in the prestigious Champions League. The differences between Dutch clubs and European top-clubs such as Manchester United, FC Barcelona, Juventus, and Bayern Munich will only get bigger when the current policy is left unchanged.

I have already made the statement that the clubs in the Netherlands can only survive internationally when their players have a high average individual quality level and the teams have a perfected team building process. These are their most important weapons in pursuit of a high performance level. This, in combination with a correct match mentality, will be important to possess in the near future.

A high individual average level can only be achieved when the youth soccer education structure is perfected even more. In the Netherlands, high profiled coaches such as Johan Cruyff and Wim Jansen have already sounded the alarm bell. Their criticism was: 'not enough talented players are being developed. Thus our educational system is not functioning properly anymore. The youth coaches are failing.'

Personally I am of the opinion that the Dutch Soccer School does not turn out a smaller number of talented players compared to before. However, this new generation does have to meet the higher demands placed on them. This is why the youth soccer development system must be perfected. Taking the above mentioned developments (internationally) into account, we have to rely even more on an excellent youth soccer development system. This system, however, is not yet up to date given the increased demands of top soccer, and that is where the problem lays. If this is what Cruyff and Jansen meant to say, then they are correct.

SOLUTIONS

To notice that there is a problem is one thing, but to come up with solutions is just as important. In this book a large number of guidelines can be found that can help in resolving the problems. The guidelines for the soccer learning process can mainly be found in chapter 5. In the further perfecting of the youth soccer system, this can be of great assistance.

At the end of this book I will make some important comments in relation to this, in the interest of the future of top-level soccer.

The talents of 2001 need more soccer tools: especially ball skills, passing and kicking, and speed of action need to be improved. Additionally, an added quality of being able to act in a team efficient manner is required. A great deal of team tactical maturity will need to be available to achieve this.

This places higher demands on the mentality of the players during training sessions. High demands are also placed on the coach in relation to his practical and theoretical knowledge and his personality qualities. This concerns all top-level coaches, at the youth, amateur and professional level. Because the coach is responsible for the team's performance he will demand even more discipline than before, both during and outside the training sessions. These are essential prerequisites to increase the above mentioned soccer tools, including an iron match mentality. In such a climate the talented player has to ripen, step by step. In our welfare state such a rock hard mental burden is not easy to deal with. Let's not even discuss the enormous salaries that are being paid to and demanded by the young players.

THE FOUNDATION

When it can be concluded that the youth soccer education needs to be further perfected, this must begin at the foundation, striving for an optimal number of 5 and 6-year-old 'talented' youngsters. This demands a sophisticated promotion policy, preferably based on national and international top performances by the club teams and national team. The 'stars', the idols of the youth, play a key role in the popularity and promotion of the sport.

When you want to increase the quality of the foundation, you must invest in the army of specifically educated youth trainers. They need to create the ideal conditions for the 6-12 year olds so the youth players can learn the game, play the game and have fun playing their favorite game. The learning process must be focused on developing those qualities that are needed to learn to play a simplified match (4v4 or 7v7), and not on - especially taking the limited hours of training into account - less important training activities for these age categories.

It is even recommended that specific trainers are educated for the different age groups. For example, for the 5-10 year olds, the 10-12, 12-14, 14-16, 16-18, and the18-21 year olds. These specifically educated trainers should mostly be former players. Though this is usually not what they aspire to do, I believe that many would be willing to take on a managerial role as a technical coordinator or director of education. This would be an important step in the right direction.

Furthermore, the talented players will have to do some daily 'homework'. The soccer learning process should not be limited to the few hours of training and matches at the club. Nearby his home he will have to develop a complete handling of the ball (Coerver-school), passing, dribbling, and heading skills. It is also a must that additional matches are played during the week. Parents can play an important role to accomplish this.

It is essential that early on young talented players come in contact with the importance of teamwork while playing a match, not through tactical instructions made by the trainer or coach. It is all about explaining to the young talent, taking his soccer age into account, that with good teamwork the chance that the team will be successful will be greater. Winning is the players' ultimate motivation, so as a coach you use that to stimulate. By internalizing simple guidelines, out of their own free will, and through coaching each other, they will achieve more. This is only a part of the training session. The central focus should remain on the individual development, thus on the individual actions of dribbling, outplaying and beating an opponent. His friends on the team will critique him during this.

More than ever the focus should be placed in the mental training in the learning process from a young age on. Naturally, growing up in a welfare state brings with it some disturbing factors concerning social discipline, dealing with sacrifices and the necessary stamina, character traits that are essential when structurally living as an athlete. Most important, of course, is the emotional challenge that occurs from playing this game. Furthermore, the daily living environment should enhance the talent development.

However it may be, the mental training and development demand great insight and feeling from parents and specific youth soccer coaches. Competitive soccer and a good training attitude demand: enjoying the game, concentration, being alert, match and training insight, positive aggression, self-control, team spirit, stamina, courage, self confidence, team discipline, taking responsibility, and discipline in life...

This is a wide range of qualities that is variegated differently for each youth player. It is the art of coaching and parenting to recognize this and to play with this. Nagging about something that will not be achieved has a counter effect. However, taking the great mental demands placed on players at the top into account, it is important to confront the players with this at a young age. Over and over again during matches and training sessions, situations occur that are suitable for "mental training". This is because these situations have emotional ballast and it concerns a hobby they enjoy. That and playing in a team make it possible for coaches to tactfully mold talented (and not-so-talented) players.

LENGTHENING OF THE LEARNING PROCESS

I would like to place an emphasis, taking the high demands placed on talented players into account, that the learning process for most players is not finished at the age of 18! To be able to cross the T's (especially mentally) it is necessary to lengthen the learning process till about 21 years old. The extra attention given to this group of 18-21 year olds is one of the necessary solutions to perfect the complete youth development! The package of higher demands is placed mostly on this age group.

In any case, it is of great importance that these young players between 18-21 years old receive an additional top-level education, linked to a top-level competitive league just for this age group. Many countries do not have such a league. The current competition in the Netherlands for B-teams of professional clubs is not sufficient. The educational process of this age group does not only demand better, accomplished coaches, but also requires a developmental top-league. Automatically, this means a better competition structure and that more investments should be made. It seems that also in this area we are falling behind in the Netherlands. This is of course a complex situation. A combination of soccer technical and political forces is required. This will cost a lot of money!

As the talent develops as a soccer player and as a person, he must be confronted with a mental "toughness" that is necessary to stay afloat under the professional pressure placed on him in the year 2001. This confrontation means that the player has to learn and accept playing with the structures of a team task and function assigned by his coach.

The talented player must realize that ups and especially downs are an integral part of the development process. To learn to sit the bench is also an educational objective. For many a young player, it would be better to ripen further in a team that has less quality, so he has better chances to play. When he has the necessary abilities, it will come out. Unfortunately such a temporary step back usually places too big a mental burden on the (top) talented player.

The professionalization is unbreakably linked to: stamina, perseverance, and making sacrifices, mental vitality to reach a goal or goals and learning to expand the boundaries of your abilities. This is not easy to do. Usually the individual has to be forced and pressured. The coach plays a key role in this process. On the basis of my experiences as a coach, I look at this as endless "fight" between the coach and the players to reach an athletic objective. Without a constant mental pressure it is difficult to get the most out of a team. Sometimes you are successful, sometimes you fail.

For the coach, team manager, and manager the identical mental attitude is necessary: do not cut corners, but take the most difficult road. Actually that is the ultimate challenge of such a process. You need players who are 'SOB's'. There is no room for compassion on the pitch. Outside the pitch the "street fighter" becomes a different person, just as is the case with soldiers at the battle lines. This survival instinct brings out forces that were unknown before. And, playing at the top-level is a battle for survival. The story that it is just a game is "bullshit". This is true even for most top-amateur players. In this atmosphere of survival there is no room for hobbying individuals. They should play at the recreational level.

Key players that are team tactically mature and have credibility are invaluable extensions of the coach during training sessions and matches. A capable professional staff is a must. The coach's right hand, his assistant coach, must be his sounding board. Below them, in soccer technical aspects, comes the second string that creates the best conditions for the coach to do his job. Unfortunately there are many people in the world of athletics that find it tough to play this role.

Psychologically this is not an easy role to play. To put your own interests behind the interest of the team is not a simple matter. It should not surprise anyone that this regularly fails to happen.

To conclude: you have read a number of guidelines in this book to aid in increasing the performance level of a team. Just like you are dependent upon the qualities and contributions of the players, the "value" of this book will depend on your dealing with and applying these guidelines. I wish you lots of success!

CURRICULUM VITAE
RINUS MICHELS

Born February 9, 1928 in Amsterdam, The Netherlands

PLAYER FOR AJAX AMSTERDAM FROM 1946-1958

Rinus Michels played five times for the National Team of the Netherlands:

June 18, 1950	Stockholm	vs Sweden	4-1W
June 11, 1950	Helsinki	vs Finland	4-1W
April 4, 1954	Antwerp	vs Belgium	4-0W
May 19, 1954	Stockholm	vs Sweden	6-1W
May 30, 1954	Zurich	vs Switzerland	3-1W

CAREER AS TRAINER

1960-1964	JOS Amsterdam (amateurs)
1964-1965	AFC Amsterdam (amateurs)
1965-1971	Ajax Amsterdam
1971-1975	Barcelona
1974	Dutch National Team Coach
1975-1976	Ajax Amsterdam (technical director)
1976-1978	Barcelona
1978-1980	Los Angeles Aztecs
1980-1983	FC Köln
1984-1986	Technical Director KNVB
1986-1988	National Team Coach of the Netherlands
1988-1989	Bayer Leverkusen
1990-1992	National Team Coach of the Netherlands

HONORS AS TRAINER

1x World Cup Final: (with The Netherlands)	1974 World Cup
1x European Champion: (with The Netherlands)	1988 European Championships
2x Final European Cup I: (now Chamions League)	1969 AC Milan - Ajax 4-1 1971 Ajax - Panathinaikos 2-0

4x National Champions with Ajax			1966, 1967, 1968, 1970			
1x National Champion with Barcelona			1974			

3x Dutch League Cup
  Champions   1967, 1970, 1971
  with Ajax
1x Spanish Cup Champion
  with Barcelona   1978
1x German Cup Champion
  with FC Köln   1983

Coach of the Century   1999

RESULTS DURING THE FOUR PERIODS AS NATIONAL TEAM COACH OF THE NETHERLANDS

	Gms	W	T	L	Pts	%
Pd 1	10	6	3	1	15	75.0%
Pd 2	3	1	0	2	2	33.3%
Pd 3	22	12	6	4	30	68.2%
Pd 4	19	11	5	3	27	71.1%
	54	30	14	10	74	68.5%

1st Period:
03-27-74   The Netherlands - Austria   1-1 Rotterdam
05-26-74   The Netherlands - Argentina 4-1 Amsterdam
06-05-74   The Netherlands - Romania   0-0 Rotterdam

World Championships in West Germany

06-15-74   The Netherlands - Uruguay   2-0   Hannover
06-19-74   The Netherlands - Sweden   0-0   Dortmund
06-23-74   The Netherlands - Bulgaria   4-1   Dortmund
06-26-74   The Netherlands - Argentina   4-0
           Gelsenkirchen
06-30-74   The Netherlands - East Germany 2-0
           Gelsenkirchen
07-03-74   The Netherlands - Brazil   2-0 Dortmund
07-07-74   The Netherlands - West Germany 1-2
           Munich

2nd Period:

10-17-84	The Netherlands - Hungary	1-2	Rotterdam
11-14-84	Austria - The Netherlands	1-0	Viena
12-23-84	Cyprus - The Netherlands	0-1	Nicosia

3rd Period:

04-29-86	The Netherlands - Scotland	0-0	Eindhoven
05-14-86	West Germany - The Netherlands	3-1	Dortmund
09-10-86	Czechoslovakia - The Netherlands	1-0	Prague
10-15-86	Hungary - The Netherlands	0-1	Budapest
11-19-86	The Netherlands - Poland	0-0	Amsterdam
12-21-86	Cyprus - The Netherlands	0-2	Limassol
01-21-87	Spain - The Netherlands	1-1	Barcelona
03-25-87	The Netherlands - Greece	1-1	Rotterdam
04-29-87	The Netherlands - Hungary	2-0	Rotterdam
09-09-87	The Netherlands - Belgium	0-0	Rotterdam
10-14-87	Poland - The Netherlands	0-2	Zabrze
10-28-87	The Netherlands - Cyprus	8-0	Rotterdam
11-17-87	The Netherlands - Cyprus	4-0	Amsterdam
12-16-87	Greece - The Netherlands	0-3	Rhodos
03-23-88	England - The Netherlands	2-2	London
05-24-88	The Netherlands - Bulgaria	1-2	Rotterdam
06-01-88	The Netherlands - Romania	2-0	Amsterdam

European Championships - West Germany

06-12-88	The Netherlands - Russia	0-1	Köln
06-15-99	The Netherlands - England	3-1	Düsseldorf
06-18-88	The Netherlands - Ireland	1-0	Gelsenkirchen
06-21-88	The Netherlands - West Ger	2-1	Hamburg
06-25-88	The Netherlands - Russia	2-0	Munich

4th Period:

09-26-90	Italy - The Netherlands	1-0	Palermo
10-17-90	Portugal - The Netherlands	1-0	Porto
11-21-90	The Netherlands - Greece	2-0	Rotterdam
12-19-90	Malta - The Netherlands	0-8	Rabat Ta'Qali
03-13-91	The Netherlands - Malta	1-0	Rotterdam
04-17-91	The Netherlands - Finland	2-0	Rotterdam
06-05-91	Finland - The Netherlands	1-1	Helsinki
09-11-91	The Netherlands - Poland	1-1	Eindhoven
10-16-91	The Netherlands - Portugal	1-0	Rotterdam
12-04-91	Greece - The Netherlands	0-2	Thessaloniki

02-12-92	Portugal - The Netherlands	2-0	Faro
03-25-92	The Netherlands - Yugoslavia	2-0	Amsterdam
05-27-92	The Netherlands - Austria	3-2	Sittard
05-30-92	The Netherlands - Wales	4-0	Utrecht
06-05-92	France - The Netherlands	1-1	Lens

European Championships - Sweden

06-12-92	The Netherlands - Scotland	1-0	Göteborg
06-15-92	The Netherlands - COS	0-0	Göteborg
06-18-92	The Netherlands - Germany	3-1	Göteborg
06-22-92	The Netherlands - Denmark	2-2 (pen 6-7) Göteborg